Food and Cooking of
CHILE

Food and Cooking of
CHILE

BORIS BASSO BENELLI
PHOTOGRAPHY BY MARTIN BRIGDALE

60 delicious recipes from
a unique and vibrant cuisine

LORENZ BOOKS

This edition is published by Lorenz Books,
an imprint of Anness Publishing Ltd
108 Great Russell Street
London WC1B 3NA; info@anness.com

www.lorenzbooks.com; www.annesspublishing.com

If you like the images in this book and would
like to investigate using them for publishing,
promotions or advertising, please visit our website
www.practicalpictures.com for more information.

A CIP catalogue record for this book is available
from the British Library.

Publisher: Joanna Lorenz
Editor: Joanne Rippin
Photographer: Martin Brigdale
Food stylists: Annie Rigg and Jayne Cross
Designer: Adelle Mahoney
Research: Lucy Doncaster

PUBLISHER'S NOTE
Although the advice and information in this book are
believed to be accurate and true at the time of going to
press, neither the authors nor the publisher can accept any
legal responsibility or liability for any errors or omissions that
may have been made nor for any inaccuracies nor for any
loss, harm or injury that comes about from following
instructions or advice in this book.

NOTES
Bracketed terms are intended for American readers.
For all recipes, quantities are given in both metric and
imperial measures and, where appropriate, in standard cups
and spoons. Follow one set of measures, but not a mixture,
because they are not interchangeable.
Standard spoon and cup measures are level.
1 tsp = 5ml, 1 tbsp = 15ml, 1 cup = 250ml/8fl oz.
Australian standard tablespoons are 20ml.
Australian readers should use 3 tsp in place of 1 tbsp for
measuring small quantities.
American pints are 16fl oz/2 cups. American readers
should use 20fl oz/2.5 cups in place of 1 pint when
measuring liquids.
Electric oven temperatures in this book are for conventional
ovens. When using a fan oven, the temperature will probably
need to be reduced by about 10–20°C/20–40°F. Since
ovens vary, you should check with your manufacturer's
instruction book for guidance.
The nutritional analysis given for each recipe is calculated per
portion (i.e. serving or item), unless otherwise stated. If the
recipe gives a range, such as Serves 4–6, then the nutritional
analysis will be for the smaller portion size, i.e. 6 servings.
The analysis does not include optional ingredients, such as
salt added to taste.
Medium (US large) eggs are used unless otherwise stated.

Page 1: Sunset on Playa los Artistas, Viña del Mar, with
  Wulff Castle and resort hotels in the background.
Page 23: A Chilean cowboy (huancho) in the
  Aconcagua valley.
Page 39: A vegetable seller in San Fernando market.
Page 53: Puerto Natales.
Page 69: Spit-roast pig, Rancagua.
Page 101 A Chilean fruit farm.
Page 121: A bar in Santiago.

Thanks to Alamy for permission to reproduce the images on
the following pages: 1, 6t, 6br 7tl, 7tr, 7b, 8b, 9t, 10tl, 10tr,
11ml, 11br, 11bl, 12t, 12bl, 12br, 13tl, 13tr, 13b, 14t, 14bl,
14br, 15bl, 15br, 18bl, 23, 39, 53, 69, 101, 121.
Thanks to Corbis for permission to reproduce the image on
page 15t.
Thanks also to the author for the image on page 8t.

Contents

Introduction

Melding traditional ingredients with Spanish and European cooking methods, Chilean cuisine makes wonderful use of the huge variety of top-quality foods the country produces, from tomatoes, maize and avocados to the range of fish and shellfish from the Pacific Ocean. These abundant ingredients, together with a love of good food and world-class wine, have resulted in a cuisine that is as varied and exciting as the country's spectacular landscape.

Left: The modern high-rise buildings of the city of Santiago are dwarfed by the towering mountain range that encircles it.

Below: The beautiful wide bay of Zapallar, on the Pacific coast.

Perhaps because it is one of the most stable Latin American countries, Chile has a thriving tourist trade that provides visitors with a huge range of activities, from skiing to surfing, wildlife watching to wine tasting. Home to both the driest place on the planet and a region with one of the highest rainfalls, the climate and topography couldn't be more varied. With wide open spaces, unique wildlife and amazing food and wine, Chile offers something for everyone.

A country of contrasts

In this land of extremes most types of topography can be found – from the lunar landscape of the Atacama desert and the vertiginous, rugged heights of the Andes, through the lush Central Valleys and the Lake District, to the Patagonian fjords and glaciers or the ice fields of Antarctica in the south. There are also rainforests containing unique and endangered species of plants and animals, and pristine beaches whose waters abound with all manner of sea life, including more than half of the world's whale species. We are very proud that the waters around Chile are designated a whale sanctuary, and people from all over the globe come to see them in their natural habitat.

In addition to tourism, another major industry is mining and exporting minerals, especially copper, and the state-run Codelco mine in

Above: Colchagua Valley is one of Chile's best-known regions for world-renowned quality red wines. The area is home to more than 30 vineyards, such as Viña Lapostolle, Viu Manent, Montes and MontGras.

Below: The Rapi Nui people of Easter Island still inhabit the place where their ancestors first raised these mysterious statues.

northern Chile is the largest copper mine in the world. But mostly importantly for the cuisine, agriculture – both subsistence and for export – is also big business, with products such as wheat, tomatoes, grapes, beans, beef, lamb and numerous other food ingredients being dispatched across the globe.

Chilean wine is increasingly popular, and with ideal conditions for viticulture, and a passion for the end product, our vineyards continue to flourish. Fishing, for food and for sport, is also important, especially along the extensive coast, or on the islands where marine produce is still a staple of the daily diet.

A rich heritage

It is believed that people have lived in the stretch of land known now as Chile since 13000BC. Archaeological excavations at Monte Verde in southern Chile have revealed evidence of settlers dating back to that time, and for centuries since then many different indigenous people lived in communities all over the country, from the deserts of the Atacama to the once thickly forested Easter Island. These early peoples left their mark in the form of amazing works of art, like the Gigante de Atacama geoglyph in the northern desert and the iconic moai of Easter Island.

Above: A fisherman in the village of Concón, north of Valparaíso displays his catch of squid, caught in the waters of the Pacific Ocean.

Following the influx of conquistadors in the 15th century, and later immigrants, these rural communities diminished, but the legacy they left is still celebrated with festivals, and an awareness of how important it is to maintain our cultural continuity. This is particularly evident in the food and cooking of Chile, where native ingredients such as maize, quinoa, squash and potatoes are given a European feel with Spanish influences and cooking methods.

About this book

Chilean food is a harmonious combination of indigenous and imported ingredients, and the selection of recipes in this volume includes many of our most iconic dishes. The book begins with an introduction that describes how history, geography and culture contribute to the story of this exciting land and its people, and also gives an overview of the nation's favourite foods. The delicious regional recipes that follow represent the time-honoured family cooking that is still found in Chilean homes. From humitas and pebre to ceviche and empanadas, recreating these dishes will take you on a tantalizing culinary journey around a breathtaking country.

Geography and climate

Situated on the western edge of South America, bordered by Peru to the north and Argentina and Bolivia to the east, Chile is notable for its long, very thin shape. It is 4,190km (2,600 miles) long but no more than 185km (115 miles) across at its widest point. The country counts Robinson Crusoe Island and the Pacific Islands among its territories.

Part of the Ring of Fire, Chile has 36 live volcanoes and many thermal hot springs. With several tectonic plate junctions under land and sea, the country is prone to earthquakes, especially in the south, including the largest earthquake ever recorded, the Valdivía quake of 1960. Other tectonic shifts in the past created the colossal Andes mountain range that runs down the eastern edge of the country, and much later were responsible for the destruction of much of the fine colonial architecture that was once found in the capital, Santiago.

Norte Grande and Norte Chico

The arid upper third of country is home to the Atacama desert, the driest place on earth. Famed for its otherworldly landscapes and unique flora and fauna, this region also has unparalleled clear skies, which means it is also popular with astronomers and scientists.

Lichens, cacti and shrubs survive on the coastal side of the region thanks to a Pacific fog called Camanchaca, and these plants provide fodder for hardy camelids such as llamas and alpacas. These, together with a range of unusual tubers, form the basis of the simple protein-rich diet in the arid areas. Warming dishes such as estofado (beef stew) and cocido de llama (llama casserole) remain strongly influenced by the traditions of the Aymara and Atacameño people of the Andes.

In the far north lies the Andean plateau where considerable rainfall occurs, meaning that some fruits and vegetables can be grown. Along the coast are the major fishing ports of Iquique and Antofagasta, where local menus feature many traditional recipes from the Chango tribe, such as cazuela marina (seafood stew) and erizos con salsa verde (sea urchin with green sauce). Pisco, a type of grape

Above: Fertile farming land in the Temuco region, also known as the Lake District.

Below: The peaks and salt lakes of the Atacama desert.

Right: Some of the distinctive houses, built on stilts, that huddle on the water's edge on Chiloé Island.

Below: The long thin shape of Chile is defined by the Andes mountains on one side and the Pacific Ocean on the other.

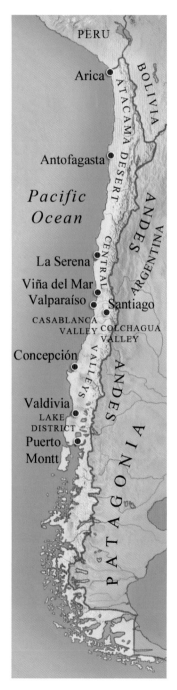

brandy, is produced in the wine valleys of the north and central regions and is a favourite drink throughout the country.

The lush Central Valleys

With a Mediterranean microclimate, and fertile land, the Central Valleys are the agricultural heartland of Chile. Conditions here are ideal for growing all manner of vegetables and fruits – including onions, wheat, corn, oats, apples, peaches and berries. The flat land nestled at the foothills of the Andes is also where Chile's vineyards produce some of the best wines in the world, especially in Colchagua Valley and Casablanca Valley.

As well as being home to the capital city Santiago, the valleys contain Valparaíso, once the South Pacific's greatest port. This maritime hillside city, together with nearby Concepción, remains one of the country's largest metropolitan areas outside Santiago.

The Lake District and Chiloé Island

Situated towards the southern end of Chile, the Lake District presents vistas of snowcapped volcanoes and sparkling lakes as well as the world-renowned Valdivían rainforest. One of the rainiest regions of the world, the abundant lush pastures are ideal for cattle farming. In addition to the stunning scenery, many lakes and freshwater rivers abound with fish such as salmon and trout, and fishing as well as tourism is big business. Many Europeans settled in this region in the mid-19th century, and the German influence in particular is reflected in local foods, especially cakes (kuchen) and desserts as well as sauerkraut.

By contrast, the nearby Chiloé archipelago is a self-sufficient region that has retained its traditions and folklore, and indigenous tribes – especially the Mapuches – still live there. Among the best-known dishes are pulmay (meat and shellfish stew), chapaleles (Chilean dumplings), valdivíano (jerky soup) and sopaipillas (pumpkin fritters). The area is also famous for its merkén or merquén, a special spice mix.

Patagonia and Tierra Del Fuego

A top tourist destination, Patagonia features a dramatic landscape of granite peaks, glacier fields, fjords and open pampas grasslands, which are home to Chile's cowboys, known as huasos, and many estancias, or ranches.

Meat – especially lamb, wild boar and venison – and fish such as salmon and trout are predominant in the local diet, and these are often smoked to preserve them for the cold winter months. The Chono dish curanto is especially iconic, and involves cooking a range of meats and vegetables on top of fire-heated stones in a deep pit.

Easter and Robinson Crusoe Islands

Most famous for its 887 statues, Easter Island, or Rapa Nui as it is called in Polynesian, is one of the remotest places on earth, lying 3,512km (2,180 miles) to the west of mainland Chile. Deforestation and overpopulation had a devastating effect on the island, but the area is now protected by UNESCO.

Robinson Crusoe Island, once known as Más a Tierra, but renamed by the Chilean government in 1966, is part of the Juan Fernández Archipelago 250km (155 miles) off the coast. Between 1704–9 the island was home to a shipwrecked sailor, Alexander Selkirk, thought to be the inspiration for Defoe's novel.

History and culture

Many of the world's favourite foods originate in Chile, including maize, potatoes, squash and beans, and these formed the basis of the diets of indigenous tribes. Culinary traditions varied according to the local landscape, and with some ethnic groups remaining relatively isolated, they retained their individual identities. The arrival of the Spanish changed everything, however, and resulted in the diverse, multicultural society and cuisine found in the country today.

Around 15,000 years ago, migrating Paleo-Indians crossed the Bering Strait via a land bridge and created the very early habitations found at Monte Verde and other excavation sites in southern and central Chile. These people flourished in the lush valleys and on the bountiful coastline, and the Mapuche people in particular became the dominant group.

By 6000BC other communities such as the Atacameños, Aymaras and Diaguitas were based in the Atacama desert and the Andean foothills in the north of the country. Once nomadic hunters who herded llama and alpaca, over time they learned how to cultivate crops and adopted a generally settled lifestyle with only sporadic seasonal movements as they herded their animals. Meat from these animals, as well as the game that was hunted, formed the basis of the diet, although some people, especially the Aymara, traded with the coastal Chango people for fish and shellfish.

In the far south, now Patagonia, lived the 'canoe Indians' – the Chono, Kawéskar and Yámana people. They survived by catching the plentiful fish and shellfish in the fjords and channels along the coast and in the Strait of Magellan. Away from the water, the Tehuelche hunted game on the Patagonian steppe while the Selk'nam (Ona) hunted on the land of the Tierra del Fuego archipelago.

Polynesian culture

Populated by settlers from eastern Polynesia some 1,000 years ago, Easter Island developed independently from mainland Chile, and has a unique cultural past. On this once densely forested island, the early people formed complex societies. However, various social and environmental changes led to deforestation, clan strife and depopulation. Numbers have recovered somewhat since then, and the Rapa Nui people now account for more than half of

Above: Two of the most ancient landscapes in Chile, to the left the Strait of Magellan, and on the right the Patagonian Steppe, still inhabited by llamas, the country's earliest herded animal.

Bottom right: A statue of Pedro de Valdivía stands in the Plaza de Armas in the centre of Santiago, the city he founded after his conquest of Chile.

Below: A little Mapuche girl wearing traditional costume.

Below: A traditional dance of the Rapa Nui being performed near Hanga Roa on Easter Island.

the current population of the island. With primarily Polynesian influences, the Pascuense cuisine of Easter Island is largely based on the huge range of seafood found around the island, including heke (octopus), pipi (sea snails) and koreh (eel); the diet also features several unique tuber varieties, poultry, pork and lamb as well as tropical fruits, bananas and coconuts. The most famous dishes are umu (a combination of meat, fish, fruit and vegetables wrapped in banana leaves and cooked in an earth oven); po'e, a banana cake; and ceviche, which is made with soy milk or coconut milk rather than juice from acidic fruits.

A time of change

Living in relative harmony for generations, the established indigenous groups on the bountiful mainland of Chile, bounded on three sides by more or less impenetrable barriers, remained safe from attack. This changed in the mid-15th century when the Incas crossed the border in the north, in a bid to conquer the continent. Having successfully taken the sparsely populated Atacama Desert, however, they were halted in their tracks by the fierce Mapuche Indians of the central areas and travelled no further south than modern Santiago.

The Incan hold on such inaccessible peripheral regions was tenuous and, following the death of their emperor Huayna Capac c.1527, a bloody civil war further loosened their grip on Chilean lands. This liberation from Incan domination in the north came at a price, leaving weakened Chilean forces vulnerable to attack from another invading force: the Spanish.

The second half of the 15th century brought about phenomenal change in what is now Latin America, as conquistadors from Spain arrived in droves. By 1494, most of Latin America was under Spanish rule. The first Spaniard to arrive in modern-day Chile was Ferdinand Magellan, who navigated the passage now known as the Magellan Strait in 1520. In 1535 Diego de Almagro unsuccessfully attempted to take over the lands, but six years later, in 1541, Pedro de

Valdivía led a victorious campaign, and went on to establish the capital Santiago as well as the cities of La Serena, Valparaíso, Concepción, Villarrica and Valdivía.

Life under colonial rule

Initial relations between the Spanish and the indigenous people were good, but they quickly soured, and the 300-year Araucanían wars began as invaders and inhabitants clashed. The conquistadors were in Latin America to find gold, and when this failed to materialize the Spaniards resorted to other ways to enrich themselves, seizing ownership of huge tracts of ancestral land and demanding payment called encomiendas. The Catholic Church made its presence felt at about the same time, converting the local people to Catholicism, and today this remains the dominant faith in the country.

The arrival of Europeans also had an effect on the Chilean diet, as Spanish settlers introduced livestock such as pigs, cattle, chickens and sheep, as well as wheat and wine. These were incorporated into the local cuisines and most classic Chilean dishes contain a combination of all of these ingredients, both old and new. Unfortunately the conquerors also brought with them disease, most notably smallpox, which tore through the indigenous tribes and devalued the encomiendas, since there

were so few people left to pay. This led to the establishment of large rural estates called haciendas, although there was little or no labour force to work on them.

As Spaniards cohabited with local women, a new ethnic group was born and given the name mestizos. This resulted in a new social order, with rich landowners appropriating the best agricultural land, while the indigenous tribes were left with the poorest territories. This issue of access to land was divisive well into the 20th century, but the more pressing matter at the time was Chile's increasing alienation from Spain, as Chilean-born Spaniards (criollos) grew to resent interference from Europe and campaigned for independence. This led to a clash between royalist Spaniards and criollos, which resulted in Chile declaring independence in 1810. After a period of civil unrest a new conservative power emerged, creating a centralized government and installing Catholicism as the state religion.

This right-wing government was pro-capitalist and pro-landowners, and their policies coincided with a boom in the economy. This was due to an increase in the number of ships stopping at the port of Valparaíso on their way round Cape Horn to California during the gold rush, and the huge demand for Chilean wheat from San Francisco. This marked the start of a phenomenal export trade and a booming shipping industry; those with power prospered.

Colonial eating habits

Meals during colonial times were often heavy, calorific affairs, with lunch the main meal of the day. This usually began with a fish, meat or poultry dish and was followed by a stew (guiso) served with corn (choclo) and one of the three most common types of bread – a soft Spanish bread made with fat; a thin, crispy Chilean bread; and an unleavened wheat bread cooked over hot coals called tortilla de rescoldo. Dessert was usually fresh fruit, and herbal tea (paico) was consumed to aid digestion. Mate, a drink containing caffeine made with the leaves of the yerba mate plant, was the hot beverage of choice in the south of the country.

As Christianity spread in the 17th century, the number of Catholic monasteries and convents increased and it was in these establishments that the tradition of pastry making became popular. Many modern treats, such as sopaipillas (pumpkin discs) and calzones rotos (pastry twists), date back to this period and Chileans still have the saying 'tiene mano de monja', meaning 'she has the hands of a nun', i.e. they are exceptionally good at baking. More foods, such as turkeys, geese, watermelons and melons arrived from Mexico and Jamaica, and the cuisine started to become more sophisticated among the ruling classes. At around the same point in the 18th century coffee started to rival mate, and Chilean wine began to be produced.

Above: Valparaíso, once an important centre of the American gold rush, is still a bustling international shipping port.

Below: The Catholic Church became an important force in Chile during the Spanish era, and built churches all over the country, from tiny altiplano adobe structures, left, to ornate urban cathedrals, right.

Above: Empanadas, warming on the barbecue, are one of the many traditional foods eaten on Independence Day.

Top right: There are wonderful food markets to be found in every town and city, such as this one in Castro, Chiloé Island.

Below: Abandoned farm buildings on Estancia San Gregorio, in Patagonia, one of Chile's huge farms now referred to as ghost ranches.

Expansion and immigration

Throughout the 19th century Chile's territories grew. To the north, parts of the Atacama region formerly held by Bolivia and Peru were seized. To the south, the Auracanian wars had made the region unstable and dangerous for immigrants, so in order to consolidate the region as part of Chile and end the fighting, the government concluded several treaties with the Mapuches. This opened up the lands south of the Bío Bío river and resulted in an influx of new settlers from Europe. The majority of these people were German, but immigrants also included Italians, English, Swiss and Croatians. Today, this Germanic influence remains strong, and can be seen in the architecture of the houses, and in the thriving dairy industry.

Decline and mass-urbanization

The start of the 20th century saw the end of Chile's boom years. Demand for minerals dwindled as synthetic versions were invented; the opening of the Panama Canal meant that ships no longer had to navigate Cape Horn and could bypass the once-thriving port of Valparaíso; and the start of World War I resulted in the abrupt cessation of trade with two of the country's major partners, Germany and Britain.

With large privatized farms monopolizing the agricultural land, many rural people moved to the cities to seek work. The gap between rich and poor widened and there were calls for the confiscation of large rural estates. In 1970, when Salvador Guillermo Allende Gossens came to power and instituted many reforms, violence ensued as landowners and workers clashed. To deal with this, Allende appointed General Augusto Pinochet Ugarte as commander-in-chief of the army. Three weeks later, Pinochet led a military coup that overthrew Allende. Chile had entered a period of military dictatorship that continued until 1989, when, following the successful and largely peaceful 'Si' to democracy campaign, an elected president took over from Pinochet.

Modern-day Chileans and food

Chile today is a multi-ethnic society with a strong and unique identity. The majority of people are of mixed Spanish and Amerindian descent, and the national language is Spanish. In the face of so much change, it is perhaps surprising that so many traditional recipes have survived. The fact that they have is largely due to the combined ancestry of the population, which has retained a memory of the old ways while also embracing colonial and more recently introduced dishes.

Country dwellers continue to eat the foods they grow or hunt locally, while in the cities the cuisine is a melting pot of influences. With so many wonderful ingredients available, urban Chileans have access to a wide range of dishes and there is a thriving restaurant scene.

Everyday eating and special festivals

Chileans are proud of the food they produce and the dishes they create with it, and no weekend is complete without the family coming together to enjoy an asado, or barbecue. With Catholicism the dominant religion, there is no shortage of saints' days and religious holidays to mark, although there is also a strong tradition of celebrating pre-Christian and indigenous festivals.

The daily rhythm

Chileans follow an eating pattern similar to that found in many parts of Europe. Desayuno, breakfast, is the lightest meal of the day and consists of bread with butter, jam or cheese, and perhaps some yogurt, fruit or cereal.

Almuerzo, or lunch, is eaten between 1pm and 4pm and is the largest meal of the day. It often involves soup, a main course, then a salad and finally a dessert. The soup varies according to the season – in summer it may be dropped. Tea time, or onces, happens around 6pm and is inherited from the British. It consists of tea, toast or cake, a kind of evening breakfast.

Dinner, or cena, is a light meal taken at about 8pm. A more substantial dinner is called comida, but this is reserved for special occasions. There is not a big snacking culture, although hot dogs topped with mashed avocado and mayonnaise are popular street food for lunch.

Below: Cordero al palo, spit-roast lamb, cooked on the traditional asado or barbecue.

Summer – a time to party

The hottest months of the year in much of Chile fall between December and February, and this is when many of the major festivals occur. With children on holiday and parents often taking the whole of February off work, many people head to the coast. There are numerous cultural events, many of which celebrate local folklore and indigenous culture, including the Tapati Rapa Nui on Easter Island; the Festival Costumbrista Chilote, which focuses on the unique local heritage and in particular traditional foods of Chiloé Island; and the Carnaval de Putre, a festival celebrating the Aymara people in the Andean region.

Noche Buena (Christmas Eve) is the big religious event of the season throughout Chile. From mid-afternoon onwards, extended families come together to swap gifts and enjoy a late dinner before attending midnight mass. The comida (dinner) usually consists of roasted meat followed by pan de Pascua, a rich, spongy fruitcake, all washed down with plenty of wine. Cola de mono (monkey's tail), a drink made with coffee, milk, brandy and spices is also traditionally drunk. Navidad (Christmas Day) itself is a quieter day, with families visiting friends or going to the beach.

Between Christmas and New Year is the week-long festival in Valparaíso celebrating the performing arts, from classical theatre and dance to cinema and parades, and all manner of food stalls. The event culminates with one of the largest firework displays in the world on Fin de Año (New Year's Eve). It is traditional to drink ponche a la Romana, a combination of champagne and pineapple ice cream.

Above: Empanadas, stuffed with beef, are eaten at every available opportunity in all parts of Chile.

Below: Choclo (cornmeal-topped cottage pie), served at a restaurant in Pomaire.

Asado

The asado, or barbecue, is an important part of weekend family life in Chile, as it is in much of Latin America. Beef, lamb, pork, goat and fish are all slow-cooked on a grill (parrilla) positioned quite high above hot coals. In Patagonia, cordero al palo (spit-roast lamb) is especially popular for special celebrations, with whole animals being roasted on a stick positioned in the ground near an open fire.

Above: A traditional Chilean vineyard in the world-renowned Colchagua Valley.

Bottom right: On All Saints Day, or Day of the Dead, people leave flowers and candles on the graves of their relatives to remember those who have died.

Below: A Chilean cowboy, the huaso, celebrating Independence Day in Santa Cruz.

Autumn festivals

In early March, the harvesting season begins, heralding the start of the wine festivals, especially in the Central Valleys. On the religious calendar, Lent and Easter are the notable events, and many Catholics abstain from eating meat on Fridays. Even people who do not observe the restrictions will usually abstain from eating meat on Viernes Santo (Good Friday). On Pascua (Easter Day) itself, also known as Resurrection Sunday, children go on Easter-egg hunts.

Winter processions

The cold temperatures in some parts of Chile between June and August bring snow, and the skiing season begins in the south. To the north of the country some of the largest festivals occur, with lively costumed processions, fireworks and dances. Food tends to be warming and hearty, and soups become a more important part of the main lunchtime meal.

One of the largest nationwide events occurs on the 29th June, the Fiesta de San Pedro. Along the coast, people pay homage to St. Peter, the patron saint of fishermen, and statues of the saint are carried in processions to the harbour in the hope of good fortune, kind weather conditions and large catches. Inland, especially in Atacama, St. Peter is celebrated as the patron saint of the Catholic Church, and this is marked with masses and costumed processions, especially in the town of San Pedro de Atacama.

Spring celebrations

Deemed by many to be the most pleasant season, weather-wise, spring in Chile brings moderate temperatures, intermittent rainfall and a glorious display of spring flowers. Between the 18th and 19th September people celebrate Fiestas Patrias – Independence Day and Armed Forces Day.

The country's heritage is celebrated nationwide on Día de la Raza (the Day of the Race, or Columbus Day) in October, with parades of ethnic groups playing traditional instruments. Día de Todos los Santos (All Saints Day) is also the Day of the Dead, when families visit cemeteries with pan de la muerto (bread of the dead) for their deceased relatives.

Chilean ingredients

The people of Chile love to eat locally sourced food, and in a country that produces such a diverse range of ingredients we are often spoilt for choice. In the major cities the ferias, or street markets, take place in different locations every day, selling fresh fruit, vegetables, meat, fish and shellfish, dairy produce and some speciality items such as palm honey or kollongka eggs. Among the many favourite ingredients are tomatoes, potatoes and fresh corn, which appear again and again in traditional recipes, along with beef or other meats, and of course Chile's wonderful wine.

Fish and shellfish

In a land with such a long, productive coastline and numerous lakes, rivers and fjords, it is perhaps not surprising that fish and shellfish have historically been so important in the nation's diet. With the vast majority of the catches now being exported, however, seafood prices are relatively high and Chileans eat less fish and shellfish than they used to, but it is still enjoyed for special occasions. Many classic dishes provide the ideal showcase for the top-quality seafood that does find its way to local markets and the caletas, or fishermen's wharves, where the day's catch can be bought.

Among the many fish loved by Chileans, congrio (conger eel) is one of the most iconic; the poet Pablo Neruda loved it so much he wrote an ode in its honour. Other substantial meaty fish appear in baked or braised dishes, including salmon and reineta (pomfret), which can be combined with chorizo and baked with cheese to make cancato. Albacora (swordfish) or atún (tuna) steaks make an ideal alternative to meat for the weekly asado, or marinated in

garlic and turmeric, pan-fried and served with a simple accompaniment of rice or potatoes and vegetables. Tinned tuna is also used and appears in the much-loved appetizer palta reina con atún (queen avocado with tuna).

Delicate fish such as merluza (hake) and lenguado (sole) are often best quickly fried in a little olive oil or butter. The nation's favourite, merluza, is usually what is served when 'fried fish' is ordered, and battered fillets are often sandwiched in a soft roll and topped with parsley and a squeeze of lemon for a tasty, quick meal. Lenguado can also be used to make the special-occasion dish, lenguado con salsa de erizos, in which fried fillets are covered with a creamy sea urchin sauce and served with rice. Ceviche, a dish of raw fish marinated in citrus juice, is made with whatever happens to be at its freshest on the day, and is extremely popular, especially on Easter Island.

The oxygen-rich waters along the coast of Chile provide the perfect conditions for shellfish, and the nation enjoys eating a wonderful variety, including locos (abalones),

Above: Fried fish sandwich, churrasco marino, is a favourite quick meal often served in coastal restaurants.

Below, from left to right: Hake, pomfret, swordfish and sea bass.

Above: Abalones, in their beautiful shells.

Below, from top to bottom: Llama, osso bucco, and beef jerky.

Preparing sea urchins

1 Protecting your hands with a thick folded cloth, turn the urchin so the circular mouth part is at the top. Use sharp kitchen scissors to pierce a hole near the edge and cut a circle round the mouth part.

2 Use a plastic spatula to lift up and remove the circle of shell, taking out the white chewing organ that is attached to the mouthpiece. Tip and pour out the liquid inside and carefully remove any black parts.

3 With a teaspoon gently scoop out the five sections of orange meat (often called the roe, but actually 'gonads'), discarding any black bits. Gently rinse the orange flesh in a bowl of cold water.

machas (Atlantic surf clams), picorocos (giant barnacles), and erizos (sea urchins), among others. These are transformed into all manner of delectable dishes, from elegant appetizers such as locos mayo (abalones with mayonnaise) to simple baked gratins as well as luxurious sauces to accompany fish, such as corvina (sea bass) con salsa margarita.

Meat and poultry

The mainstay of the diet in many regions for centuries, meat and poultry consumption in Chile has doubled in the last couple of decades as fish prices have increased. Eaten at least once a day, they appear in many classic dishes, such as cazuela, empanadas and estofado.

In the arid north, hardy camelids such as alpaca and llama have traditionally been made into warming stews, and although other meat is now available these local animals remain important, especially among the remaining indigenous groups. Elsewhere, locally sourced beef is enjoyed in many forms, from grilled (broiled) ribs and the calorie-laden chorillana to slow-cooked dishes made from osso bucco or jerky, and empanadas made with minced (ground) beef. Large cuts of beef such as asado de tira (short ribs) and steaks are the preference for the weekly barbecue, and the top-quality produce is simply seasoned and then slow-cooked over a low heat so that the full flavour of the meat is brought out.

Introduced by the Spanish, lamb was once the major meat eaten by the Mapuche people in the south and appeared in soups and stews such as cazuelas, carbonadas and pucheros as well as cordero al palo (spit-roasted lamb). Today, despite the many sheep that are reared, lamb plays a minor role in the nation's diet, and the majority of the prime cuts are exported. Pork, however, in its many forms – from chops and ribs to chorizo and smoked sausages – is more popular and features in favourites such as tomaticán and pulmay (meat and shellfish stew) as well as alongside the large cuts of beef on the asado.

White meat such as chicken, turkey and rabbit is often marinated and then slow-cooked, although chicken wings, thighs and drumsticks sometimes appear on the parilla, or grill, alongside the steaks, burgers and ribs. Pollo arvejado (chicken and pea casserole) is a popular one-pot dish in Chilean homes, providing a quick and easy meal of meat and

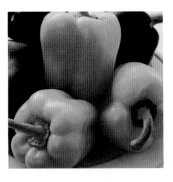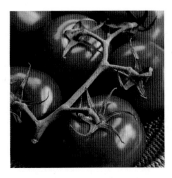

vegetables. The Araucana or Mapuche breed of chicken is a species that is endemic to southern Chile, and in addition to having flavoursome meat it is notable for the lovely light blue-green eggs the birds produce.

Dairy products and eggs

Introduced by immigrants, especially the Germans who settled in the Lake District region in the mid-19th century, dairy herds now graze the prime grasslands in southern Chile, especially between Valdivía and Puerto Montt. Along with milk, products include cheese, butter and cream, the latter of which are used to make the delectable kuchen and milk-based desserts such as leche asada (Chilean-style baked milk pudding) and leche nevada (snow milk) that Chileans so enjoy. Cheese was unknown in Chile until the 19th century and does not feature in traditional recipes. However, in typical Chilean fashion it has been incorporated into old recipes and appears in gratinated shellfish dishes.

Eggs are used in all manner of ways, both savoury and sweet, including tortilla – made with shellfish or fish, green beans, peas or anything else that is to hand – and on top of chorillana. They are also used to make mayonnaise, which is served with locos for an appetizer as well as being liberally applied to fast food such as hotdogs and churrasco Italiano (beef, tomato and avocado sandwich).

Vegetables

One of the world's major exporters of vegetables, Chile produces and enjoys a magnificent range of top-quality ingredients, ranging from asparagus, beans, olives and tomatoes to corn, avocados, onions and garlic. Many of these new crops were introduced by European settlers, but prior to their arrival indigenous people cultivated a great range of vegetables, and trade between farmers and fishermen was commonplace. Possibly the most important of these native crops was maize or corn, known as choclo in Chile, which fuelled the mighty Maya, Aztec and Inca empires. Having been spread across the country from the Atacameños in the north to the Mapuches in the south by traders, maize still features in many national favourites, such as humitas (Chilean tamales), pastel de choclo (corn pie) and porotos granados (corn and bean stew).

Above, from left to right: Chile's most popular vegetables, (bell) peppers, tomatoes, avocados and corn.

Bottom left: Cattle graze on the fertile pastures beneath the active volcano of Villarrica.

Below, from top to bottom: Humitas and porotos granados.

Above: Sopaipillas, little fritters made from mashed pumpkin.

Right: Pumpkin is a favourite ingredient in Chilean soups, stews and even sweet dishes.

Below: Merquén is ground, smoked chilli pepper, which is added to many recipes.

Bottom right: Cinnamon sticks are used to flavour sweet drinks and desserts.

Tubers, including potatoes but also varieties that are more or less unknown outside Chile and some that are unique to Easter Island, were key to survival in harsh conditions, and potatoes still appear in many stews and casseroles or are mashed, roasted, boiled or fried to provide a sustaining accompaniment to a great range of other dishes.

Squash, especially pumpkin, is a popular ingredient, and a delectable soup made from baked pumpkin, which is served in the hollowed-out shell, makes an eye-catching dish. The popular snack sopaipillas (pumpkin discs) are a common feature at festivals, and chunks of the bright flesh appear in many stews and casseroles. Spaghetti squash is combined with sugar and transformed into a delectable conserve that is used for spreading on bread or topped with walnuts and eaten on its own.

Among the rainbow of seasonal vegetables, including (bell) peppers, courgettes (zucchini), beans, cabbages, peas, avocados and any number of other types, tomatoes in particular are a Chilean favourite. Combined with mild, sweet onions in the form of pebre (Chilean salsa) and ensalada Chilena (Chilean tomato and onion salad), these side dishes appear at every asado and alongside any number of other dishes, especially fried fish, where their fresh flavours and bright colours perfectly complement the mild-tasting fish.

Herbs and spices

Chileans use herbs and spices carefully in their cooking, as flavour-enhancers rather than as dominant features. The most commonly used ones are dried oregano and ground cumin, which, along with salt and pepper, are the primary seasoning agents. Paprika and merquén or merken (ground, smoked chilli pepper) lend a spicy note to dry rubs for meat and fish, in lentil and vegetable dishes, in stews and pies, and on peanuts and salty olives. Primarily used in Mapuche and other Andean cuisines, there are two types: 'merquén natural', which is mixed with salt, and 'special merquén',

which is a blend of merquén, salt and roasted ground coriander seeds. A small amount of fresh chilli is occasionally added to some dishes for a subtle kick, but very hot recipes are not the norm. Garlic, however, is used along with onion in numerous dishes, adding its distinctive Mediterranean flavour to traditional ingredients.

Sweet spices, such as cloves, cinnamon and nutmeg feature in the beloved milk desserts and some cakes. They are also an integral part of the fabulous Christmas drink cola de mono (monkey's tail), an eggnog-like concoction of milk, rum and spices, served ice-cold.

Fruit, nuts and seeds

Chileans eat a lot of fruit and it is usually the dessert of choice after most meals. On Easter Island, various types of banana were once a crucial part of the diet and Rapa Nui cake is still a favourite dessert. Coconuts are also abundant there and along other coastal regions, and the milk is used on Easter Island in place of lemon juice for making ceviche. Elsewhere, especially in the verdant central plains, cherries, oranges, lemons, figs, papaya, peaches and, of course, table and wine grapes grow in abundance, and these are enjoyed fresh, juiced, dried or candied for use in sweet and savoury dishes when the fruit is not in season. Cactus fruit (called tuna fruit by Chileans) is very popular, and enjoyed all over the country.

Nuts and seeds provided a very useful source of protein for indigenous people, and piñones from the araucaria, or monkey puzzle tree, were important to the Mapuche people. The seeds, similar to pine nuts, can be toasted or boiled, used to make soup or ground into flour. Almonds, walnut and chestnuts are also used in desserts, such as higos rellenos con almendras (figs stuffed with almonds) and turrón de vino (wine nougat).

Storecupboard staples

Before the introduction of wheat by the Spanish, the major crops in Chile were corn and quinoa, and these ingredients remain an important part of the diet. In addition to the fresh forms of the products, processed goods such as quinoa flour, polenta and cornmeal are also used, and appear in pastry and cakes in place of wheat flour. Wheat berries, also found in Eastern European cooking, are used in Chile for risotto and to make a nutritious dessert, with a nutty flavour and chewy texture.

Above, from left to right: Coconut, cherries, figs and papaya.

Below, from left to right: Wheat berries, almonds and monkey puzzle nuts.

Mulled wine

This drink is very popular in southern Chile. Warming for both the body and soul, its consumption can be used as a good reason for meeting friends and having a good time. Very easy to make, this recipe will serve 6 people.

1 Put 200g/7oz/1 cup sugar, 2 cinnamon sticks, and 6 cloves in a large pan, together with 250ml/8fl oz/1 cup hot water. Add 2 medium oranges, cut into thin slices, reserving a few slices for serving. Bring to the boil over a high heat and boil for 5 minutes, stirring occasionally.

2 Reduce the heat to medium and add 1.5 litres/2½ pints/6¼ cups red wine. Stir until the mixture comes back to the boil. Remove from the heat and leave to stand for a few minutes. Serve in six warmed, heatproof glasses garnished with a fresh orange slice.

Dried lentils and beans are important foods, especially in remoter regions, and the beloved puré de porotos (bean purée) shows how pulses can be transformed into satisfying meals.

For a touch of sweetness, nothing beats the unique and complex flavour of palm honey, but other sweetening agents include chañar fruit syrup and the beloved manjar, or dulce de leche, used as a filling for cakes and pastries.

Drinks

In addition to their world-class wines, Chileans drink a wide range of beverages including pisco (a type of grape brandy), pipeño (sweet fermented wine), beer, rum and many fruit juices and other soft drinks, along with mate, tea and coffee. As well as appearing in various cocktails, shots of pisco are often drunk neat, or infused with flavours from fruits such as cherries. Dried as well as fresh fruits appear in non-alcoholic beverages such as mote con huesillos (dry peaches with wheat berries), a refreshing summer drink/dessert that is enjoyed around the country.

Chilean wine

It was the Spanish who introduced the grape variety *vitis vinifera* to Chile in the mid-16th century, and with an ideal climate and perfect soil conditions in some regions, this 'black grape' or Pais variety was soon widely planted. Spain, however, placed strict limitations upon the amount of wine that could be made locally and banned exportation to other countries in an attempt to keep control of the market. Preferring their own wine to the vinegary imported versions, many Chileans ignored these strictures and grew Muscatel, Mollar and other grape varieties, which were for the most part turned into sweet, concentrated wines, pisco and aguardiente (brandy).

As Spanish authority waned, wealthy Chilean landowners visited France and brought back Cabernet Sauvignon, Merlot, Carmenère, Sauvignon and Sémillon vines – an act that helped to save some of these varieties from extinction after the phylloxera epidemic of the 1850s ravaged French vineyards. Chile's signature grape is Carmenère, a rich and popular varietal, which has a natural fruity spiciness.

Chilean wines continued to develop as vineyard owners experimented with alternative techniques, although little was exported until the end of the 20th century. This all changed in the 1980s when new technology improved the product dramatically. The wine increased exponentially. Today, Chile is among the world's largest exporters of top quality wine.

Below: A selection of the dried beans that are used in many Chilean soups and stews.

Appetizers and Sides

Chileans didn't adopt the Spanish tradition of tapas, but there are a few little dishes that are an important part of a meal, accompanied by a glass of good local red wine.

Fish and papaya ceviche
Ceviche chileno

This dish originates in the north of Chile, where the rich waters abound with all manner of sea food. Quick to prepare, ceviche in Chile is primarily composed of white fish and peppers, but the addition of fresh-tasting papaya in this version adds a delicate scented note that perfectly complements the other flavours. Any white fish can be used, but it must be very very fresh.

1 Use a fish knife or tweezers to remove any bones from the fish, then cut the fish into 2.5cm/1in cubes and put it into a bowl.

2 Finely dice the onion and peppers, and add to the fish, then finely chop the fresh coriander or parsley and stir into the fish mixture.

3 Squeeze the lemons and strain the juice if necessary to remove any pips. Add the lemon juice and sugar to the bowl.

4 Peel the papaya and cut into 1cm/³⁄₄in cubes. Add to the bowl along with the cumin, olive oil, salt and pepper. Stir gently to combine, without breaking up the papaya or fish.

5 Cover and leave to marinate in the refrigerator for a minimum of 1 hour, gently stirring the mixture every 15 minutes.

6 To serve, gently lift cubes of fish and papaya and arrange on small serving plates. Top with a spoonful of onion and peppers and drizzle some of the dressing over the top.

Cook's tip To skin fish fillets, lay the fillet on a cutting board, skin-side down. At the narrower tail end, make a cut between the skin and the flesh that is deep enough so that you can grasp the skin with your other hand. Put your knife at a 45-degree angle to the cutting board, grip the skin with your other hand and simply hold the knife while you pull the skin with your other hand. Rinse the fish. The pressure of the water should be just strong enough to remove loose scales. Pat dry with kitchen paper.

Serves 4

500g/1¼lb white fish, such as flounder, Atlantic croaker, tilapia, or mahi mahi, filleted and skinned (see Cook's tip)

1 medium onion

¹⁄₃ each of a red, a green and a yellow (bell) pepper

a small handful of fresh coriander (cilantro) or parsley

5 lemons

30ml/2 tbsp sugar

½ papaya

30ml/2 tbsp ground cumin

45ml/3 tbsp olive oil

salt and black pepper

Energy: 288kcal/1205kJ; Protein 24g; Carbohydrate 18g, of which sugars 17g; Fat 14g, of which saturates 2g; Cholesterol 0mg; Calcium 176mg; Fibre 3g; Sodium 72mg

Sea urchins with green sauce
Erizos con salsa verde

Erizos, or sea urchins, are a part of Chilean culinary history and have been plentiful along its coastline for centuries. They have a sweet, rich and creamy taste and melt in the mouth, making them a luxurious choice for a special appetizer. Using white pepper instead of black in this recipe complements the intensity of the shellfish.

1 Wearing gloves, or using a thick, folded cloth to protect your hands, carefully cut off the top of the urchins using a pair of scissors.

2 Run a rubber spatula around the inside of the shells then remove the orange flesh with a teaspoon. See page 17 for more instructions.

3 Wash the orange sacs thoroughly in water, drain and arrange in a serving bowl.

4 Mix together the onion, parsley, lemon juice, olive oil, salt and pepper in a separate bowl. Add the mixture to the sea urchins and stir until combined. Serve with lemon wedges.

Serves 4

4 fresh sea urchins

1 onion, finely chopped

30ml/2 tbsp finely chopped fresh parsley

100ml/3½fl oz/scant ½ cup lemon juice

60ml/4 tbsp olive oil

salt and white pepper

lemon wedges, to serve

Energy 178kcal/735kJ; Protein 6g; Carbohydrate 3g, of which sugars 3g; Fat 16g, of which saturates 2g; Cholesterol 173mg; Calcium 16mg; Fibre 1g; Sodium 38mg

Lentil, green beans and pine nut salad
Ensalada de lentejas con porotos verdes y piñones

Serves 4

225g/8oz/1 cup green lentils

150g/5oz/1 cup pine nuts in their shells, or 75g/2½oz/½ cup ready-prepared pine nuts

450g/1lb/3 cups green beans

For the dressing

45ml/3 tbsp olive oil

5ml/1 tsp wine vinegar

15ml/1 tbsp mustard

salt and black pepper

The Araucanía Region in southern Chile is home to the Mapuches, where this recipe originates. The Mapuches continue to follow a very natural way of life on their land, and have retained their traditions for growing and making food. Packed with pine nuts and beans, this easy recipe can be served as an appetizer or light lunch.

1 Soak the lentils in cold water overnight. Drain well, then transfer to a large pan, cover with cold water and boil for 20–25 minutes, until tender. Drain well and leave to cool.

2 Place the pine nuts in their shells in a pan with 1 litre/1¾ pints/4 cups lightly salted water. Bring to the boil and cook for about 45 minutes, until the shells begin to open.

3 Drain and leave to cool slightly, then remove the nuts from their shells. This cooking and shelling process is not necessary if you use ready-prepared pine nuts.

4 Cut the beans into 2cm/¾in lengths. Cook them in a pan of salted water for 7–8 minutes, or steam if you prefer for 8–10 minutes, until tender. Drain in a colander and rinse them under cold running water to cool rapidly and stop the cooking process.

5 To make the dressing, whisk together the oil, vinegar, mustard, salt and pepper in a large serving bowl.

6 Add the lentils, pine nuts and green beans to the bowl and mix well to combine. Serve at room temperature.

Energy 459kcal/1917kJ; Protein 21g; Carbohydrate 33g, of which sugars 5g; Fat 28g, of which saturates 2g; Cholesterol 0mg; Calcium 88mg; Fibre 3g; Sodium 155mg

Little beef turnovers
Empanadas

These small pastry turnovers are probably the most quintessentially hispanic South American food, and are eaten all over Chile, especially during the national celebrations on the 18th September. What makes Chilean empanadas unique is the filling, called pino, which comprises meat, raisins, hard-boiled egg and olives. You can find them in every neighbourhood and every food store.

Serves 4

For the beef filling

45ml/3 tbsp olive oil

1 medium onion, diced

1 garlic clove, finely chopped

250g/9oz minced (ground) beef

2.5ml/½ tsp ground cumin

10ml/2 tsp sweet paprika

5ml/1 tsp sugar

5ml/1 tsp plain (all-purpose) flour

a handful of raisins

1 hard-boiled egg, peeled and cut into 8 wedges

8 olives, pitted and cut in half

salt and black pepper

For the dough

225g/8oz/2 cups plain (all-purpose) flour

2.5ml/½ tsp baking powder

2 egg yolks

100ml/3½fl oz/½ cup white wine

25g/1oz/1 tbsp butter

50ml/2fl oz/¼ cup semi-skimmed (low-fat) milk

5ml/1 tsp salt

1 First, make the filling. Heat the oil in a frying pan, add the onion and garlic and sauté over a medium heat for 8–10 minutes, until translucent. Increase the heat and add the beef. Cook, stirring, for 5 minutes, until the meat is browned.

2 Season the meat mixture with ground cumin, sweet paprika, salt and pepper. Cook for a further 3 minutes, then add the sugar and flour and cook for 2 minutes more. Remove the pan from the heat and leave the mixture to cool.

3 Meanwhile, make the dough. Sift the flour and baking powder on to a work surface. Make a well in the middle and add one egg yolk, a sprinkle of salt and the white wine. Mix all the ingredients thoroughly using your hands.

4 Heat the oven to 180°C/350°F/Gas 4. Put the butter and milk in a small pan over a low heat. When the butter has melted, slowly add enough of the liquid to the flour and egg mixture to make a soft dough, you may not need it all. Knead for 5 minutes, until smooth.

5 Divide the dough into eight even-size balls and roll out to a thickness of 5mm/¼in on a lightly floured surface.

6 Place 10ml/2 tsp of meat, a few raisins, a piece of hard-boiled egg and two olive halves in the middle of each dough round. Moisten the edges with warm water, fold the pastry to make a semi-circle and press the edges together.

7 Brush the empanadas with the remaining egg yolk, place on a baking tray and bake for 15 minutes, until golden-brown. Serve warm.

Energy 554kcal/2319kJ; Protein 23g; Carbohydrate 55g, of which sugars 10g; Fat 28g, of which saturates 9g; Cholesterol 198mg; Calcium 144mg; Fibre 3g; Sodium 814mg

Pumpkin fritters
Sopaipillas

These golden discs are very popular throughout Chile, especially in winter, when they are made on rainy afternoons. Made with wheat flour, mashed pumpkin and butter, and fried in oil, sopaipillas are often enjoyed with a cup of coffee as a midmorning snack. They can also be eaten with beer as an aperitif, or served to children as a dessert, sprinkled with chancaca (soft dark brown sugar).

1 Cook the diced pumpkin in a large pan of boiling water for 10–15 minutes, until tender. Drain, then mash it with a fork.

2 Sift the flour and baking powder into a large mixing bowl, then add the pumpkin and salt.

3 Place the milk and butter in a pan over a medium heat and heat for about 3 minutes until the butter melts.

4 Gradually add the milk and butter to the mixing bowl, stirring well between each addition, to combine thoroughly.

5 Transfer the dough to a lightly floured surface and knead it for 10 minutes, or until the mixture no longer sticks to the surface.

6 Use a rolling pin to roll out the dough until it is 5mm/¼in thick. Use a glass or a cookie cutter to cut the dough into circles that are about 6cm/3in in diameter. Prick the circles with a fork so the holes go all the way through the dough.

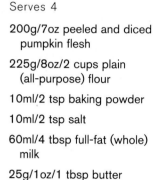

7 Heat the oil in a large, deep frying pan to 190°C/375°F. Carefully lower in a few dough circles at a time and deep-fry for 1 minute on each side, turning them with a slotted spoon. They should be brown, but not dark.

8 Carefully lift them out and drain on kitchen paper. Keep the cooked sopaipillas warm while you cook the remaining dough circles in the same way. Serve warm.

Serves 4

- 200g/7oz peeled and diced pumpkin flesh
- 225g/8oz/2 cups plain (all-purpose) flour
- 10ml/2 tsp baking powder
- 10ml/2 tsp salt
- 60ml/4 tbsp full-fat (whole) milk
- 25g/1oz/1 tbsp butter
- 500ml/17fl oz/generous 2 cups vegetable oil, for deep-frying

Energy 348kcal/1459kJ; Protein 6g; Carbohydrate 46g, of which sugars 2g; Fat 17g, of which saturates 5g; Cholesterol 15mg; Calcium 135mg; Fibre 2g; Sodium 1265mg

Chilean dumplings and salsa
Chapaleles y chancho en piedra

Especially popular in the cuisine of Chiloé Island, chapaleles are usually served with a meat and seafood soup called pulmay. In this version, created by the indigenous Huilliches from the Valdivía Province, it is served with chancho en piedra, 'pig in stone', a delicious tomato dip that actually derives its name from the verb chancar, meaning 'to grind', and refers to the process of making the dip.

Serves 4–6

1kg/2¼lb potatoes

50g/2oz bacon lardons

25g/1oz/¼ cup plain (all-purpose) flour

25g/1oz/1 tbsp butter

1 egg, beaten

salt

vegetable oil, for frying

For the chancho en piedra

3 ripe tomatoes, roughly chopped

1 clove garlic

1 medium onion, finely chopped

2 green chillies, finely chopped

30ml/2 tbsp olive oil

salt and black pepper

1 Peel the potatoes and cut them into even chunks. Place them in a large pan of boiling water and boil for 20 minutes, until soft.

2 Drain the potatoes well, allowing the steam to dissipate and the potatoes to dry out, then return them to the pan and mash them, or pass through a potato ricer into a large bowl.

3 Meanwhile, dry-fry the lardons in a hot frying pan over a medium-high heat for 3–4 minutes, until cooked. Drain and leave to cool.

4 Add the flour, butter, bacon, egg and salt to the potato. Stir to combine, until a soft dough forms. If the mixture becomes sticky, add some more flour. Transfer to a lightly floured surface and press it out using your hands until it is 2–3cm/¾–1¼in in thick. Cut into rectangles.

5 Heat the oil in a deep pan suitable for deep-frying until it reaches 190°C/375°F. Add the chapaleles and fry in batches for 4–5 minutes, until they are golden brown, carefully turning with a slotted spoon half way through cooking.

6 Place the cooked chapaleles on kitchen paper and keep warm while you cook the rest.

7 To make the chancho en piedra, place the tomatoes and garlic in a mortar and pound them with a pestle, until they are crushed and well combined but not too smooth.

8 Add the chopped onion and chillies to the mortar, season with olive oil, salt and pepper to taste, and combine everything well. Transfer to a serving dish. Serve the chapaleles while they are hot, topped with a spoonful of salsa.

Energy 258kcal/1081kJ; Protein 7g; Carbohydrate 35g, of which sugars 4g; Fat 11g, of which saturates 3g; Cholesterol 51mg; Calcium 30mg; Fibre 4g; Sodium 168mg

Avocado stuffed with tuna
Palta reina con atún

Serves 4

2 ripe but firm avocados

juice of ¹/₂ lemon

1 x 165g/5¹/₂oz can tuna, drained

1 roasted red (bell) pepper in oil, drained and diced

15ml/1 tbsp olive oil, plus extra for drizzling

115g/4oz/¹/₂ cup mayonnaise

15ml/1 tbsp Dijon mustard

1 hard-boiled egg

a few black olives, pitted

8 lettuce leaves

salt and black pepper

Cheap and plentiful in Chile, avocados are eaten at breakfast and teatime with slices or chunks of bread. Creamy, delicious and nutritious, they are also used to make this wonderfully simple appetizer, which is served on a bed of lettuce.

1 Peel the avocados and cut them lengthwise into halves. Brush or rub the avocados with the lemon juice and then set aside while you prepare the filling.

2 In a bowl, combine the tuna, red pepper, olive oil, mayonnaise, mustard, salt and pepper. Mix gently to maintain the shape of the ingredients. Mash the hard-boiled egg in a separate dish with a fork.

3 Slice the pitted olives. Place two lettuce leaves on each of four plates.

4 Stuff the cavities of each avocado half with the tuna mixture and garnish on the top with a little mashed egg and a few sliced olives.

5 Place the avocado halves on top of the lettuce leaves. Drizzle over a few drops of olive oil on to each and serve immediately.

Energy 455kcal/1881kJ; Protein 11g; Carbohydrate 5g, of which sugars 4g; Fat 43g, of which saturates 8g; Cholesterol 86mg; Calcium 29mg; Fibre 1g; Sodium 143mg

Quinoa salad
Ensalada de quinoa

Quinoa is referred to as the wheat of the Incas, and is native to the Andes. Word has spread around the world, and it is now appreciated for its high protein and nutritional value. It has a slightly nutty flavour and a similar texture to couscous.

1 Wash the quinoa thoroughly by swirling it with your fingers in a large bowl of cold water, then leave it to soak for 1 hour. Strain.

2 Heat 15ml/1 tbsp of oil in a large pan over a low heat. Add the quinoa and fry for 2 minutes.

3 Add 750ml/1¼ pints/3 cups boiling water and season with salt and pepper. Cover the pan and cook for 15–20 minutes or until the quinoa is soft. Remove from the heat, fluff up the grains using a fork and set aside.

4 Heat the remaining olive oil in a frying pan over a medium heat. Add the carrot, celery and pepper and fry for 5 minutes, until softened.

5 Meanwhile, make the dressing by combining the ingredients well, either in a bowl with a whisk or in a screw-top jar.

6 Transfer the fried vegetables to a large bowl, then add the warm quinoa, avocado, tomato, seasoning and the dressing. Combine thoroughly and serve, garnished with coriander.

Serves 4

250g/9oz/1½ cups white quinoa

30ml/2 tbsp olive oil

1 carrot, peeled and diced

2 celery sticks, diced

1 red (bell) pepper, diced

1 avocado, diced

1 tomato, deseeded and diced

salt and ground black pepper

fresh coriander (cilantro), to garnish

For the dressing

30ml/2 tbsp olive oil

7.5ml/1½ tsp balsamic vinegar

salt and black pepper

Energy 422kcal/1762kJ; Protein 10g; Carbohydrate 40g, of which sugars 9g; Fat 25g, of which saturates 4g; Cholesterol 0mg; Calcium 69mg; Fibre 5g; Sodium 58mg

Chilean salsa
Pebre

A pebre is a spicy salsa made with raw vegetables and flavoured with a spice blend called merquén. This spice mix is made from a chilli pepper of Mapuche origin, which is ground and lightly toasted and mixed with crushed coriander seeds. Pebre is found on almost every table in Chile and accompanies many dishes.

1 Pour the olive oil into a bowl. Peel and finely dice the onion, then place it in a colander, mix in the sugar then wash under warm running water. This process will help to make the taste of the onion less raw and astringent. Add the onion to the bowl.

2 Finely chop the coriander. Peel and dice the tomato and deseed and finely chop the chilli, if using. Add all of these to the bowl, along with the merquén, the vinegar and the lemon juice.

3 Season the mixture with cumin, black pepper and salt and stir well to combine.

4 Cover and leave to marinate in the refrigerator for 2–3 hours, but bring back to room temperature to serve.

Cook's tip To peel the tomato, score an 'X' at the top. Immerse in a bowl of just-boiled water for 1 minute, then remove to a bowl of cold water. The skin should now come away easily.

Serves 4

45ml/3 tbsp olive oil

1 medium onion

15ml/1 tbsp sugar

1 bunch of fresh coriander (cilantro)

1 large tomato

1 green chilli, optional

15ml/3 tsp merquén (see page 96)

15ml/1 tbsp white wine vinegar

juice of 1/2 lemon

5ml/1 tsp ground cumin

5ml/1 tsp black pepper

5ml/1 tsp salt

Energy 131kcal/541kJ; Protein 1g; Carbohydrate 7g, of which sugars 6g; Fat 12g, of which saturates 2g; Cholesterol 0mg; Calcium 16mg; Fibre 1g; Sodium 17mg

Tomato and onion salad
Ensalada chilena

Serves 4

4 tomatoes

1 onion

1 green chilli

For the dressing

50ml/2fl oz/¼ cup olive oil

15ml/1 tbsp wine vinegar

salt and black pepper

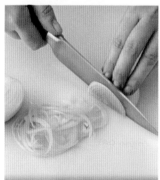

This salad is served at every Chilean barbecue and is the preferred accompaniment to fried fish, although it is delicious served with most dishes. The onions should be very finely sliced a la pluma ('like feathers'), and left to marinate with all the other ingredients so that the raw taste is reduced slightly.

1 Peel the tomatoes (see the Cook's tip opposite). Cut into slices.

2 Peel the onion and cut it in half, then crossways into thin slices. Cut the green chilli into small cubes. Remove the chilli seeds if you prefer.

3 Place the tomatoes, onion and chilli in a serving bowl and dress with olive oil, vinegar, salt and pepper.

4 Stir, cover and leave to marinate for 15 minutes. Serve the salad at room temperature.

Energy 29kcal/122kJ; Protein 1g; Carbohydrate 6g, of which sugars 5g; Fat 0g, of which saturates 0g; Cholesterol 0mg; Calcium 16mg; Fibre 2g; Sodium 9mg

Soups

Filling, sustaining soups, made from plenty of vegetables, were an important part of the rural diet, and are still enjoyed today. In the winter months Chilean soups help to keep the cold at bay.

Conger eel soup
Caldillo de congrio

This classic fish soup from the Chilean coast became known to the wider world thanks to the Chilean poet Pablo Neruda, who wrote an ode to the dish, *Oda al Caldillo de Congrio*. Conger eel can be difficult to find, but you can substitute monkfish tail for similarly delectable results.

Serves 4

600g/1lb 6oz conger eel

1 tomato

45ml/3 tbsp vegetable oil

1 onion, peeled and finely sliced

1 carrot, peeled and cut into julienne strips

1 red (bell) pepper, finely chopped

1 green chilli, finely chopped (deseeded if preferred)

10ml/2 tsp paprika

5ml/1 tsp dried oregano

200ml/7fl oz/scant 1 cup white wine

2 potatoes, peeled and chopped into small pieces

15ml/1 tbsp lemon juice

salt and black pepper

crusty bread, to serve

For the stock

½ onion, peeled

2 carrots, cut into large pieces

2 celery stalks, cut into large pieces

1 sprig of fresh coriander (cilantro)

5 garlic cloves, peeled

6 bay leaves

2 litres/3½ pints/8 cups water

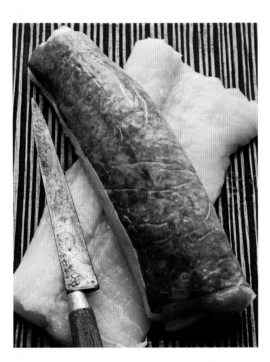

1 First, prepare the conger eel. Using a sharp knife, remove and reserve the head. Slice off the flesh from either side of the backbone, to form long fillets. Reserve the backbone. Dip your fingers in salt, for better grip, then pull off the skin from the fillets. Discard. Cut each fillet into two pieces and remove any bones.

2 Place the eel's head and the backbone in a large pan along with all the stock ingredients. Boil for 40 minutes then remove the eel and strain, reserving the stock.

3 Remove the skin from the tomato by scoring a cross at the top with a sharp knife and placing the tomato in a small bowl of boiling water for 30 seconds. Transfer to a bowl of iced water for about 1 minute, then remove and peel off the skin, deseed and finely chop.

4 Heat the oil in a large pan and add the onion, carrot, pepper and chilli. Gently fry over a medium heat for about 5 minutes, until slightly softened. Add the paprika, oregano, wine and 1 litre/1¾ pints/4 cups strained fish stock.

5 Season the eel fillets with salt and add to the pan along with the potato, tomato, lemon juice and seasoning to taste. Cook for 8 minutes, or until the fish is opaque and cooked through.

6 Ladle the soup into warmed bowls, ensuring each person receives a fillet. Serve with fresh, crusty bread.

Energy 386kcal/1613kJ; Protein 30g; Carbohydrate 25g, of which sugars 11g; Fat 19g, of which saturates 1g; Cholesterol 225mg; Calcium 150mg; Fibre 5g; Sodium 108mg

Clam soup
Sopa de machas

Clams have long been an important part of the diet on the Pacific coast of Chile. The large clams that are caught here are notable for the shape of the curved white shell that contrasts with the flesh, which turns a delicate pink colour during cooking. Any other kind of clams can be used.

1 Melt the butter in a large pan over a low heat, then add the onion and sauté for 3 minutes.

2 Add the clams and the thyme, and season with salt and pepper. Stir to combine, then add the white wine.

3 Bring to a simmer and cook for 3–5 minutes, until the clams open. Remove the clams with a slotted spoon and transfer them to a bowl, discarding any that fail to open.

4 Add the potatoes to the pan of stock, along with 1.5 litres/2½ pints/6¼ cups water. Bring to a simmer, then cook over a low heat for 20 minutes, until the potatoes are cooked.

5 Meanwhile, when the clams are cool enough to handle, remove them from the shells.

6 Allow the cooked potatoes to cool down for a few minutes, then transfer them to a blender with two thirds of the clams and a little of the cooking liquid. Blend until smooth, then gradually add the rest of the cooking liquid.

7 Pour the mixture back into the pan and heat gently for 3 minutes. Stir in the cream and most of the remaining clams, heat without allowing it to boil, then pour into soup bowls, garnish with parsley and a couple of the remaining clams and serve.

Serves 6

50g/2oz/¼ cup butter

1 onion, finely diced

40 clams

1 sprig of fresh thyme

200ml/7fl oz/scant 1 cup white wine

800g/1¾lb potatoes, peeled and diced

200ml/7fl oz/scant 1 cup single (light) cream

fresh parsley, to garnish

salt and black pepper

Cook's tip Clams must be live when cooked. Rinse them under cold running water to remove any grit. Check that the shells are undamaged and tightly shut (or close tightly when tapped) just before cooking.

Energy 334kcal/1396kJ; Protein 21g; Carbohydrate 29g, of which sugars 3g; Fat 15g, of which saturates 9g; Cholesterol 81mg; Calcium 105mg; Fibre 3g; Sodium 145mg

Turkey broth with polenta
Cazuela de pava con chuchoca

This traditional dish can be enjoyed all year round, although it is commonly eaten during winter in Chile. Polenta, made from coarsely ground corn, and packed with energy and nutrition, is a favourite ingredient in Chilean cuisine. It is very often used as a thickening ingredient for soups and stews as well as a side dish.

1 Put the turkey thighs and 1.75 litres/ 3 pints/7¹/₂ cups salted water into a large pan and boil for 45 minutes, until the meat is tender. Skim the surface with a large spoon to remove any residue that rises to the top.

2 Add the sliced onion, potatoes and carrots to the pan, then stir in the polenta.

3 Continue cooking, stirring constantly, for a further 15–20 minutes, until the potatoes and carrots are tender but not collapsing.

4 Test for seasoning; as there is no stock in this recipe you might need some more salt. Ladle into warmed soup bowls and garnish with fresh coriander.

Serves 6

6 turkey thighs

1 onion, sliced

675g/1¹/₂lb potatoes, peeled and sliced

4 carrots, sliced

5 tbsp/75ml polenta

1 small bunch fresh coriander (cilantro), to garnish

salt

Energy 289kcal/1218kJ; Protein 16g; Carbohydrate 48g, of which sugars 3g; Fat 4g, of which saturates 1g; Cholesterol 52mg; Calcium 27mg; Fibre 4g; Sodium 32mg

Barbecue soup
Ajiaco chileno

Serves 4

45ml/3 tbsp vegetable oil

2 onions, sliced

5ml/1 tsp paprika

1 garlic clove, finely chopped

5ml/1 tsp fresh oregano

5ml/1 tsp ground cumin

675g/1½lb potatoes, peeled and cut into strips

450g/1lb leftover roasted beef, cut into strips

1 green chilli

30ml/2 tbsp finely chopped fresh parsley

3 hard-boiled eggs, sliced into rounds

salt

This is a tasty and comforting soup that is ideal for cold winter days. It is often served on Mondays as a means of using up leftovers from the traditional Sunday barbecue that is enjoyed in most parts of Chile. The soup can also be made with the leftovers of a joint of beef roasted in the oven.

1 Heat the oil in a large pan over a medium heat, then add the sliced onions. Sauté the onions for about 5 minutes, until softened.

2 Stir in the paprika, garlic, oregano and cumin and cook for 2–3 minutes, until the garlic has softened slightly, then add the potatoes and the sliced beef.

3 Cook, stirring occasionally, for 10 minutes, or until the mixture is browned.

4 Add 1 litre/2 pints/5 cups of boiling water to the pan and cook, uncovered, for 30 minutes.

5 Remove the seeds from the chilli and slice it lengthways into thin strips. Add the chilli and the chopped parsley to the pan at the end of the cooking time.

6 To serve, place slices of hard-boiled egg in the bottom of each soup dish, then ladle the soup on top.

Energy 539kcal/2256kJ; Protein 50g; Carbohydrate 35g, of which sugars 5g; Fat 23g, of which saturates 5g; Cholesterol 243mg; Calcium 59mg; Fibre 4g; Sodium 137mg

Veal soup with dumplings
Pantrucas

This popular Chilean soup contains little dumplings, made from an egg-enriched dough that is cut into rectangles and cooked in meat broth to produce a tasty and invigorating soup. It used to be served to 'skinny misses' before church services, so they wouldn't feel faint during the long prayers.

Serves 6

1kg/2¼lb osso bucco (see Cook's tip)

1 onion, cut into quarters

1 garlic head, cut in half

1 red (bell) pepper, cut into quarters

15ml/1 tbsp fresh or dried oregano

1 sprig of fresh coriander (cilantro)

1 egg yolk

15ml/1 tbsp finely chopped fresh parsley

salt and black pepper

For the dough

115g/4oz/1 cup plain (all-purpose) flour

a pinch of salt

120ml/4fl oz/½ cup warm water

1 Put the osso bucco in a large pan and cover with 1.75 litres/3 pints/7½ cups water. Add the onion, garlic, red pepper, oregano, fresh coriander, salt and pepper and bring to the boil. Simmer over a medium heat for 45 minutes.

2 Strain the stock into a clean pan. Discard all of the vegetables and the bones. Cut the cooked meat into small cubes.

3 To make the dumplings, put the flour and salt into a bowl, then add enough of the warm water to make a soft and elastic dough. Turn it out on to a lightly floured board and roll it out into a rough rectangle that is about 5mm/¼in thick. Cut the dough into 2 x 4cm/¾ x 1½in rectangles.

4 Heat the strained soup over a medium heat until it is boiling. Gently add the dough rectangles to the boiling soup and cook them for 5–8 minutes, until they float to the surface. Add the cubes of meat to heat through.

5 Lightly beat the egg yolk, then divide it between six deep warmed soup bowls. Add a small portion of chopped parsley to each bowl, then ladle the boiling soup on top and serve.

Cook's tip Osso bucco, an Italian name meaning 'bone with a hole', are veal shins that can be found in most good butchers. The bone marrow in the middle melts during the long, slow cooking, adding an intense richness and depth of flavour, and thickening the sauce.

Energy 304kcal/1287kJ; Protein 49g; Carbohydrate 18g, of which sugars 2g; Fat 5g, of which saturates 2g; Cholesterol 138mg; Calcium 47mg; Fibre 1g; Sodium 121mg

Beef and vegetable broth
Carbonada

Serves 4

30ml/2 tbsp olive oil

450g/1lb chuck steak, diced

1 large carrot, diced

½ onion, chopped

2 cloves garlic, finely chopped

5ml/1 tsp dried oregano

5ml/1 tsp paprika

3 medium potatoes, peeled and diced

150g/5oz/1 cup diced pumpkin

45ml/3 tbsp long grain rice

150g/5oz/1 cup green beans, cut in half

115g/4oz/1 cup peas

salt and black pepper

Chilean beef soup is served in a deep dish, either with plenty of broth or almost dry, according to the personal preference of the diners. The vast majority of Chileans, whether they live in rural or urban areas, appreciate good-quality, healthy and nutritious food, and this ethos is much in evidence in this traditional broth.

1 Heat the oil in a large pan over a high heat, then add the diced steak. Season with salt and pepper and brown for about 5 minutes.

2 Reduce the heat to medium, then add the carrot, onion, garlic, oregano and paprika to the pan and continue sautéing for 10 minutes, until the vegetables are softened.

3 Add 1.75 litres/3 pints/7½ cups boiling water and cook, uncovered, for 45 minutes.

4 Stir the potatoes, pumpkin and rice into the broth, and cook for 15 minutes.

5 Add the green beans and the peas and cook for a further 5 minutes, until all the vegetables are cooked through. Add seasoning if needed, then ladle into deep serving bowls and serve.

Cook's tip You can adjust the amount of liquid you add according to how much broth you prefer and how intense you like the flavour.

Energy 392kcal/1644kJ; Protein 31g; Carbohydrate 35g, of which sugars 7g; Fat 15g, of which saturates 4g; Cholesterol 71mg; Calcium 64mg; Fibre 1g; Sodium 121mg

Beef jerky soup
Valdiviano

This soup dates back to when Pedro Gutiérrez, a Spaniard later known as Pedro de Valdivía, conquered the city of Valdivía in 1552. The recipe was created when dried meat was the only kind available, as cattle had not yet reached this far-flung territory, and comprises a simple mixture of local and long-lasting ingredients.

1 Preheat the oven to 230°C/450°F/Gas 8. Place the jerky on a baking sheet and toast it in the oven for 10 minutes, until crispy. Allow to cool slightly, then break it into little strips.

2 Heat the oil in a large pan over a medium heat, then add the sliced onions and sauté for 5 minutes, until tender but not browned. Stir in the paprika. Add the jerky pieces, oregano and cumin and stir to combine.

3 Dissolve the stock cube in 1 litre/2 pints/7½ cups boiling water.

4 Add the stock to the pan and boil everything for 1 hour. Stir in the chilli, parsley and the orange juice and season to taste with salt.

5 Poach the eggs by breaking them into a large spoon or ladle, one at time, and carefully lowering into the pan of simmering soup. Cook for 2–3 minutes.

6 Carefully remove the eggs with a slotted spoon once they are poached, and place each one in a separate soup bowl. Ladle over some soup and garnish with parsley to serve.

Serves 6

225g/8oz dried beef jerky

60ml/4 tbsp vegetable oil

4 onions, sliced

10ml/2 tsp paprika

5ml/1 tsp dried oregano

a pinch of ground cumin

1 beef stock (bouillon) cube

1 hot green chilli, seeded and finely chopped

15ml/1 tbsp chopped fresh parsley, plus extra for garnish

juice of 1 bitter orange

6 eggs

salt

Energy 376kcal/1566kJ; Protein 22g; Carbohydrate 14g, of which sugars 7g; Fat 27g, of which saturates 7g; Cholesterol 256mg; Calcium 71mg; Fibre 2g; Sodium 1096mg

Pumpkin soup
Sopa de zapallo

There are many types of pumpkin in Chile, and they are often named after the city where they are grown. This recipe is prepared with sweet pumpkin, which is the most widely used variety and has a large quantity of dense flesh.

1 Preheat the oven to 190°C/375°F/Gas 5. Cut off the top part of the pumpkin, so that it can be used as a lid. Clean the inside of the pumpkin, removing all the fibres and seeds.

2 Brush the inside of the pumpkin with oil, replace the pumpkin top, place on a baking tray and cook in the oven for 20 minutes.

3 Meanwhile, melt the butter in a large pan over a medium heat, then add the leeks, carrot and celery. Cook for 8 minutes, until softened.

4 Add the beef stock to the pan, bring to the boil, then add the tomatoes, salt and pepper.

5 Place the rice, bay leaves and the vegetable soup mixture inside the pumpkin and cover with the top. Cook in the oven for 1 hour.

6 Take the pumpkin out of the oven and remove the lid. Add the cream to the soup, season, then ladle the liquid into bowls. Cut some of the pumpkin flesh from the walls, add to each bowl and garnish with parsley.

Serves 4

1 whole pumpkin, weighing about 4kg/9lb

30ml/2 tbsp olive or vegetable oil

50g/2oz/¼ cup butter

2 medium leeks, trimmed, cleaned and sliced

1 medium carrot, grated

2 celery stalks, sliced

1 litre/1¾ pints/4 cups beef stock

250ml/8fl oz/1 cup peeled, seeded and finely chopped tomatoes, or canned chopped tomatoes

65g/2½oz/⅓ cup long grain rice

2 bay leaves

250ml/8fl oz/1 cup double (heavy) cream

salt and black pepper

45ml/3 tbsp finely chopped fresh parsley, to garnish

Energy 610kcal/2530kJ; Protein 7g; Carbohydrate 28g, of which sugars 12g; Fat 53g, of which saturates 29g; Cholesterol 112mg; Calcium 181mg; Fibre 5g; Sodium 384mg

Monkey puzzle seed soup
Sopa de piñones

Serves 4

250ml/8fl oz/1 cup milk

1kg/2¼lb monkey puzzle nuts with skins removed (see Cook's tip), or 200g/7oz pine nuts or blanched almonds

15ml/1 tbsp chopped fresh coriander (cilantro)

15ml/1 tbsp olive oil

salt and black pepper

Revered as sacred by the Mapuche people, the monkey puzzle tree provides seeds that have been an important part of the diet for centuries. Known as piñones, the seeds are highly nutritious and are eaten whole, or ground to make flour. The seeds are hard to find outside Chile, so pine nuts or blanched almonds can be substituted.

1 Put the 475ml/16fl oz/2 cups water with the milk in a pan and heat until just boiling.

2 Grind the nuts in a pestle and mortar, or pulse in a food processor to a fine paste.

3 Add the nut paste to the milk mixture and season with salt and pepper to taste. Process briefly to combine and reheat gently.

4 Ladle into soup bowls, sprinkle with a little chopped coriander and add a few drops of oil.

Cook's tip In Chile, piñones come with the skins on. If you are able to find them, they need to be prepared to remove the skins. To do this, place them in a pan with water to cover and boil for 1 hour. Drain well, then rub the piñones in a clean dish towel to remove any remaining skin.

Energy 369kcal/1528kJ; Protein 13g; Carbohydrate 6g, of which sugars 6g; Fat 33g, of which saturates 3g; Cholesterol 4mg; Calcium 196mg; Fibre 6g; Sodium 34mg

Fish and Shellfish

Chileans make good use of their extensive coastline and eat a wide variety of deliciously fresh fish and shellfish in their diet.

Sole with sea urchin sauce
Lenguado con salsa de erizos

Serves 6

50g/2oz/2 tbsp butter, plus extra for frying

15ml/1 tbsp plain (all-purpose) flour

475ml/16fl oz/2 cups milk

2 sea urchins, prepared (see page 17)

75ml/5 tbsp double (heavy) cream

6 sole fillets, each weighing about 225g/8oz

15ml/1 tbsp olive oil

salt

cooked rice and lemon or lime wedges, to serve

Sole is a highly valued fish in Chilean cuisine. Because it has a delicate and delicious flesh it is most often very simply pan-fried in butter, but here an unusual sea urchin sauce gives the dish a rich and unique finish that complements the fine flavour and aroma of the sole.

1 Prepare a white sauce by melting the butter in a pan over a medium heat. Add the flour, stir to form a paste and cook for about 2 minutes. Remove from the heat.

2 Beat a splash of milk into the paste, then another, and return the pan to the heat. Continue adding the milk little by little, whisking well, until the mixture is creamy and thick.

3 Transfer the sauce to a blender. Add the sea urchins and cream, and process until smooth.

4 Add salt to taste to the sauce, then cover so that no skin forms, and keep warm.

5 Season the fish fillets. Place the oil and a generous knob of butter in a large frying pan and heat over a medium heat. When the butter is foaming, add the fish and cook for 3 minutes, turn over and cook for another 3 minutes.

6 Transfer the fish to warmed plates and cover with the warm sauce. Serve immediately with some cooked rice and lemon or lime wedges.

Energy 393kcal/1642kJ; Protein 44g; Carbohydrate 6g, of which sugars 4g; Fat 22g, of which saturates 12g; Cholesterol 242mg; Calcium 144mg; Fibre 0g; Sodium 323mg

Baked salmon
Cancato de salmón

This is a traditional recipe from Chiloé Island, which lies in the Pacific Ocean to the south of Chile. Reliant on fish for centuries, salmon is the most popular catch for the Chilotes (as inhabitants of the island are called), and in this warming, sustaining dish, the fish is baked in a foil parcel with chorizo, onion and cheese.

1 Prepare four 20cm/8in squares of foil and brush each with a little oil. Preheat the oven to 180°C/350°F/Gas 4.

2 Place one salmon fillet in the middle of each piece of foil. Place a few slices of onion, tomato, chorizo and cheese on top. Season with oregano, rosemary, salt and black pepper.

3 Bring up the sides of the foil and seal well at the top to create a neat package.

4 Place the packages on the baking sheet and cook for about 20 minutes, until the salmon is cooked through and opaque and the cheese is melted. Serve with buttered boiled potatoes and a green salad.

Serves 4

30ml/2 tbsp olive oil

4 salmon fillets

1/2 onion, finely sliced

2 tomatoes, sliced

1 smoked chorizo sausage, cut into slices

4 slices of mild Cheddar cheese

10ml/2 tsp dried oregano

5ml/1 tsp chopped fresh rosemary

salt and black pepper

potatoes and salad, to serve

Energy 603kcal/2504kJ; Protein 51g; Carbohydrate 2g, of which sugars 2g; Fat 43g, of which saturates 13g; Cholesterol 129mg; Calcium 268mg; Fibre 0g; Sodium 393mg

Fried fish sandwich
Churrasco marino

This is the most traditional and best-loved recipe in the city of Coquimbo, a busy port since 1840. It is so popular that the sandwich even has its own festival, at which about 1,500 of the sandwiches are devoured. The status of Churrasco Marino as the dish of the area is due to its low cost, rapid preparation and great taste.

1 First, make the batter. Put the flour and salt in a large bowl and make a 'well' in the middle. Whisk the eggs, 120ml/4fl oz/½ cup water and the oil in a separate bowl, then add a little to the well in the flour. Stir well to incorporate and make a smooth paste, then gradually whisk in the remaining liquid to form a smooth batter.

2 To make the onion salsa, mix together the sliced onion, parsley, lemon juice and salt in a bowl, and set aside while you fry the fish.

3 Heat the oil over a high heat in a large frying pan, until it is sizzling hot. Dip the hake fillets in the batter mixture, then place them in the pan. Fry the fish for 2–3 minutes, then carefully turn them over using a metal spatula and fry for 2–3 minutes on the other side, until golden and crispy. Drain well on kitchen paper.

4 Slice open the rolls or buns and fill each with a fish fillet and a spoonful of the onion mixture. Serve immediately.

Serves 4

1 onion, very finely sliced

10ml/2 tsp chopped fresh parsley

juice of 2 lemons

30ml/2 tbsp vegetable oil

4 hake fillets

4 large soft rolls or burger buns

salt

For the batter

115g/4oz/1 cup plain (all-purpose) flour

5ml/1 tsp salt

2 eggs

5ml/1 tsp vegetable oil

Energy 500kcal/2091kJ; Protein 48g; Carbohydrate 26g, of which sugars 3g; Fat 23g, of which saturates 3g; Cholesterol 58mg; Calcium 86mg; Fibre 2g; Sodium 743mg

Diamond fish with sautéed vegetables
Reineta con vegetales

Serves 4

60ml/4 tbsp olive oil

1 courgette (zucchini), cut into thin strips

1 carrot, cut into thin strips

75g/3oz portobello (field) mushrooms, sliced

5ml/1 tsp lemon juice

45ml/3 tbsp beansprouts

4 diamond fish or tilapia fillets

60ml/4 tbsp mayonnaise

50g/2oz/1 cup fresh breadcrumbs

handful of fresh basil leaves, torn

salt and black pepper

Over the last few years, diamond fish has become Chile's favourite fresh fish. It is caught in the Valparaíso area, where the local port provides the majority of the fish for market. The fish is delicious, with very firm flesh that is ideal for baking. The more internationally available tilapia is a good substitute.

1 Preheat the oven to 180°C/350°F/Gas 4. Heat 30ml/2 tbsp of the olive oil in a frying pan over a medium heat. Add the strips of courgette and carrot and sauté for 2 minutes.

2 Add the sliced mushrooms, lemon juice and beansprouts and cook for 3 more minutes. Remove from the heat.

3 Drizzle the remaining olive oil in a baking dish and arrange the fish fillets on top.

4 Spread 15ml/1 tbsp mayonnaise on the surface of each fillet. Season and then sprinkle breadcrumbs over each fillet.

5 Place in the oven and cook for 10 minutes until the fish is just cooked and the breadcrumbs are golden.

6 While the fish is in the oven, gently reheat the sautéed vegetables and stir in the torn basil leaves. Serve the fish with the vegetables.

Energy 536kcal/2233kJ; Protein 47g; Carbohydrate 10g, of which sugars 4g; Fat 34g, of which saturates 5g; Cholesterol 15mg; Calcium 335mg; Fibre 2g; Sodium 295mg

Sea bass with margarita sauce
Corvina con salsa margarita

The city of Concón, just north of Valparaíso on the Chilean coast, is known for its epic festival of sea bass each summer. This special gastronomic event sees over 20 restaurants prepare delicious corvina dishes, like this one, for more than 2,000 visitors. The sauce here is not the same as the tomato-based Italian Margherita sauce, but is a deliciously creamy accompaniment that goes perfectly with most fish.

1 Preheat the oven to 180°C/350°F/Gas 4. Place the sea bass fillets in a baking dish with the olive oil. Season with oregano, garlic, cumin, salt and black pepper.

2 Cover the baking dish with foil and bake for 20 minutes, until the fish is opaque.

3 To prepare the scallops, open the shells with a small knife, being careful not to break them. Wash them in a strainer under running cold water to remove any sand. You should have about 200g/7oz flesh, including the white flesh and the coral.

4 Shell the prawns, keeping the tail intact with the shells on. Using a small knife, remove and discard the black line that runs along the back of the prawns. You should now have about 200g/7oz prepared prawns.

5 Heat the oil over a medium heat in a large frying pan. Add the onion, red pepper and garlic, and reduce the heat to low.

6 Sauté the onion and red pepper mixture for about 10 minutes, stirring, until the onion is translucent and the pepper is soft.

7 Add the scallops, prawns and squid and stir gently to combine. Add the oregano, white wine and salt and increase the heat to medium. Cook for about 5 minutes, until the wine has reduced by about half.

8 Combine the cornflour with 120ml/4fl oz/$\frac{1}{2}$ cup water in a small bowl, then add to the frying pan along with the cream. Reduce the heat to low and cook, stirring, for 2 minutes, until it thickens. Take care not to let the cream boil.

9 Serve the fish on warmed plates with the sauce spooned over, together with equal portions of seafood. Serve with rice and salad or some crusty bread.

Cook's tip You can ask a fishmonger to prepare the scallops, prawns and squid for you.

Serves 4

4 large sea bass fillets

60ml/4 tbsp olive oil

10ml/2 tsp fresh oregano leaves

4 garlic cloves, finely chopped

10ml/2 tsp ground cumin

salt and black pepper

For the sauce

500g/1¼lb scallops

400g/14oz whole prawns (shrimp)

30ml/2 tbsp olive oil

½ onion, finely chopped

½ red (bell) pepper, diced into cubes

2 garlic cloves, finely chopped

200g/7oz prepared squid, cut into rings

10ml/2 tsp dried oregano

250ml/8fl oz/1 cup white wine

10ml/2 tsp cornflour (cornstarch)

250ml/8fl oz/1 cup double (heavy) cream

rice or crusty bread, and salad, to serve

Energy 1026kcal/4275kJ; Protein 99g; Carbohydrate 11g, of which sugars 4g; Fat 65g, of which saturates 26g; Cholesterol 640mg; Calcium 490mg; Fibre 1g; Sodium 616mg

Tuna and aubergine with Chilean rice
Atún y berenjenas y con arroz graneado

The tuna caught in Chile is fished close to Easter Island, some 2,000km/1,250 miles from the mainland. Tuna from this region has a distinctive colour and flavour, and is used to make a range of stunning dishes. This simple recipe showcases the quality of the fish and uses just a few complementary ingredients. Arroz graneado is Chile's favourite way of serving rice, and is the accompaniment for many meat and fish dishes.

Serves 4

2 large aubergines (eggplant)

60ml/4 tbsp olive oil

115g/4oz/½ cup butter

2 large tomatoes, peeled and chopped

1 sprig of fresh thyme

4 tuna steaks, around 1kg/2¼lb in total

salt and black pepper

For the arroz graneado

30ml/2 tbsp vegetable oil

2 cloves garlic, finely chopped

1 small carrot, grated

250g/8oz/1 cup long grain rice

½ red (bell) pepper, finely chopped

a handful or two of frozen peas

salt

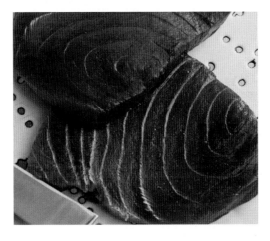

1 Preheat the oven to 180°C/350°F/Gas 4. Slice the aubergines into even slices about 1cm/½in thick.

2 Lightly brush both sides of the aubergine slices with about 15ml/1 tbsp of the olive oil and season with salt. Place on a baking tray and cook in the preheated oven for about 4–5 minutes, until golden-brown.

3 Turn the aubergine slices and cook on the other side for 3–4 minutes until tender and brown patches have appeared on the surface. Remove from the heat and set aside.

4 For the arroz, place a large pan on a medium heat, add the oil and stir-fry the garlic for a few seconds. Add the carrot and the rice and stir to coat the grains in the oil.

5 Pour 500ml/1 pint/2 cups water into the pan, add the chopped pepper and peas, and season with salt. Bring to the boil, cover, reduce the heat to very low, and simmer for 15–20 minutes until the water is absorbed.

6 Meanwhile, heat the butter in a small pan over a medium heat, add the chopped tomato and sauté for 5 minutes, until softened. Add the thyme to the pan, and cook for a few minutes more to reduce any liquid.

7 Heat a griddle, or heat the remaining oil in a frying pan, over a high heat and add the tuna steaks. Cook until golden on each side; around 7 minutes for well done or 3–4 minutes for rare, per side. Season with salt and pepper.

8 Fluff up the cooked rice with a fork. Transfer the tuna to warmed serving plates, then spoon some of the buttery tomatoes over each tuna steak. Serve with the aubergine slices and rice.

Energy 1045kcal/4371kJ; Protein 67g; Carbohydrate 62g, of which sugars 7g; Fat 61g, of which saturates 22g; Cholesterol 131mg; Calcium 103mg; Fibre 7g; Sodium 307mg

Iquique-style swordfish
Albacora frita iquiqueña

Albacora is a popular fish with a meaty texture, making it an ideal alternative to steak for the weekend barbecue in Chile. The fish grows rapidly, and reaches a length of 1.5 metres/1½ yards and a weight of about 45kg/100lb by 2 years of age. It is usually found, and fished, some miles offshore on the Pacific coast, and this dish is a speciality from the regional port of Iquique.

1 Make a marinade by stirring together the turmeric, garlic and vinegar in a bowl.

2 Season the swordfish steaks with salt and pepper. Dip both sides in the marinade, then place in a dish, cover and set aside in a refrigerator for a couple of hours so that the fish absorbs the flavours.

3 Meanwhile, boil the potatoes in their skins for 15 minutes, then drain. Leave to steam and cool slightly, then slice into thick rounds.

4 Heat 45ml/3 tbsp olive oil and the butter in a large frying pan, then add the potatoes and sauté over a medium heat for about 10 minutes, until golden, turning gently half way through cooking, taking care not to break up the potatoes. Season and keep warm.

5 Pour 15ml/1 tbsp of the oil into a frying pan, place over a high heat, then add the fish and fry for 2–3 minutes on each side, until the fish is just cooked through.

6 Serve the fish on warm plates topped with pan juices, and with lemon wedges alongside. Sprinkle the sautéed potatoes with parsley, and serve with the fish.

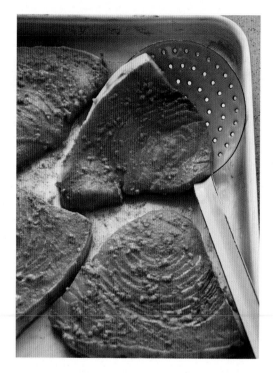

Serves 6

30ml/2 tbsp ground turmeric
3 garlic cloves, crushed
10ml/2 tsp red wine vinegar
6 swordfish steaks
900g/2lb potatoes
60ml/4 tbsp olive oil
25g/1oz/2 tbsp butter
15ml/1 tbsp chopped fresh parsley, to garnish
lemon wedges, to serve
salt and ground black pepper

Energy 508kcal/2127kJ; Protein 49g; Carbohydrate 26g, of which sugars 1g; Fat 24g, of which saturates 6g; Cholesterol 111mg; Calcium 24mg; Fibre 2g; Sodium 362mg

Barnacle gratin
Picorocos gratinados

Barnacles are curious crustaceans that look almost like a bird's beak in a shell. They grow to a great size along the coast of Chile and have an extraordinary marine-rich flavour. Infant barnacles are mobile, but the adults remain trapped in their shells and tightly fixed to the rocks, making them very easy to find and harvest. Cook in individual gratin dishes and serve with bread, salad and a cold beer!

Serves 6

12 giant barnacles

75g/3oz/3 tbsp butter, plus extra for greasing

7.5ml/1½ tsp plain (all-purpose) flour

250ml/8fl oz/1 cup white wine

2 onions, finely chopped

a pinch of nutmeg

45ml/3 tbsp grated Parmesan cheese

120ml/4fl oz/½ cup double (heavy) cream

2 egg yolks

10ml/2 tsp paprika

a little milk, if required

salt and black pepper

crusty bread and a green salad, to serve

1 Clean the barnacles by scrubbing the shells with a stiff brush under cold running water. Rinse out any sand. Place them in a large pan cover with just-boiled water and cook them for 20 minutes, until the barnacle flesh starts to fall out of the shells.

2 Carefully lift out the barnacles from the water using a slotted spoon. Cut the membrane that attaches the beak to the shell with a fine, sharp knife. Strain the cooking liquid into a bowl.

3 Gently remove the barnacle flesh, starting from the tip, and taking care not to break up the delicate flesh. Remove the little stomach sac in the centre. Leave to cool.

4 Set aside six of the barnacles with their beaks intact, and break the remaining six into chunky pieces.

5 Melt 50g/1oz/2 tbsp of the butter in a pan over a medium heat. Add the flour and cook a few minutes without browning. Add the white wine and half the cooking liquid.

6 Cook the sauce for 3–4 minutes, stirring, until it thickens, adding more stock as needed.

7 Preheat the oven to 180°C/350°F/Gas 4. Heat the remaining butter in a pan, add the onions and cook, stirring frequently, over a medium-high heat for 5 minutes, until soft.

8 Add the onions to the sauce, along with a little salt, pepper, nutmeg and 30ml/2 tbsp of the grated Parmesan.

9 Combine the cream, egg yolks and paprika in a small bowl, then add to the sauce along with the chopped barnacle flesh. Add some more stock or milk if the sauce is too thick.

10 Butter six gratin dishes. Evenly distribute the barnacle sauce between them, then place a whole barnacle in the centre of each. Sprinkle the remaining Parmesan on top.

11 Place the gratin dishes in the hot oven and cook for 15–20 minutes, until the top is golden. Serve with bread and salad.

Energy 372kcal/1539kJ; Protein 19g; Carbohydrate 6g, of which sugars 3g; Fat 30g, of which saturates 14g; Cholesterol 232mg; Calcium 94mg; Fibre 1g; Sodium 440mg

Baked clams with Parmesan
Machas a la parmesana

Serves 4

24 Atlantic surf clams, chilled

50g/2oz/4 tbsp butter

60ml/4 tbsp white wine

60ml/4 tbsp double (heavy)
cream

200g/7oz/2¹⁄₃ cups grated
Parmesan cheese

salt and black pepper

This recipe was created 50 years ago in Viña del Mar by an Italian immigrant who decided to try adding cheese to grilled clams, and liked the result. Since then it has become a classic Chilean dish and is served all over the country.

1 Preheat the oven to 180°C/350°F/Gas 4. Open the clam shells with a sturdy knife. The clams consist of a body and a muscular 'tongue'. Only the tongue is needed here.

2 Wash the tongues under running cold water to remove any sand, then gently pound the flesh with the handle of a knife and trim off any black parts. Scrub the shells and reserve half.

3 Put the 24 shell halves in a baking dish and place a little butter and a clam's tongue in each. Season with salt and black pepper.

4 Add 2.5ml/¹⁄₂ tsp white wine, a trickle of cream and a small piece of butter to each shell. Sprinkle each with grated Parmesan cheese.

5 Place in the preheated oven and cook for 5–7 minutes, until the cheese has melted. Serve immediately.

Variation If you cannot find Atlantic surf clams, you can use scallops instead.

Cook's tip The discarded clam trimmings make a delicious addition to a fish soup.

Energy 421kcal/1748kJ; Protein 28g; Carbohydrate 2g, of which sugars 1g; Fat 34g, of which saturates 21g; Cholesterol 134mg; Calcium 567mg; Fibre 0g; Sodium 1177mg

Abalones with mayonnaise

Locos mayo

Locos, as they are called in Chile, or abalones, are native to the Pacific Ocean. Universally loved for their flavour and consistency, these water snails feature on the menus of many restaurants, as well as being enjoyed at home.

1 To prepare the abalones, 'pop' the shell with a heavy knife. Starting at the shallow end and taking care not to pierce the guts, carefully slice away the flesh from the shell with a sharp knife. Remove the foot and trim off the black 'lips'. Carefully slice off the guts with a circular motion. Dispose of the foot, 'lips' and guts.

2 Pound the abalones with a heavy metal mallet, until the flesh feels soft. Scrub the beaten abalones under running water. Place in a pan with water to cover.

3 Boil the abalones for 45 minutes, until tender. Allow to cool in the water, then drain.

4 Place two abalones each on six plates. Top each with a teaspoon of mayonnaise and surround with lettuce. Garnish with a dusting of paprika, tomato strips and a lemon wedge.

Cook's tip To prepare the abalones ahead, wait until they have cooled then transfer them, with their cooking liquid, to a lidded container. Store in the refrigerator for up to 12 hours.

Serves 6

12 fresh abalones

225g/8oz/1 cup mayonnaise

2 Baby Gem (Bibb) lettuces, shredded

a few strips of tomato

3 lemons, cut into wedges, to serve

a little paprika, for dusting

Energy 440kcal/1822kJ; Protein 30g; Carbohydrate 11g, of which sugars 1g; Fat 30g, of which saturates 5g; Cholesterol 173mg; Calcium 60mg; Fibre 0g; Sodium 681mg

Main Dishes

As in other South American countries meat, especially beef, is a much-loved part of the Chilean diet. Main courses do include vegetarian dishes, however, influenced by pre-colonial ingredients.

Chicken with tomatoes and almonds
Pollo con tomate y almendras

Tomatoes in Chile are large and plump and, like so much of the amazing fresh fruit and vegetables grown throughout the country, are always full of delicious flavour. Adding almonds to the tomatoes and chicken makes this warm, hearty, winter dish go a little further, served with rice and a green salad.

Serves 6

50g/2oz/½ cup plain (all-purpose) flour

1 chicken, jointed into six pieces (see Cook's tip, or you can ask a butcher to do this for you)

25g/1oz/2 tbsp butter

30ml/2 tbsp vegetable oil

250ml/8fl oz/1 cup white wine

2 large tomatoes, peeled and cut in half

15–30ml/1–2 tbsp fresh oregano

50g/2oz/½ cup flaked (sliced) almonds

salt and black pepper

boiled rice and a green salad, to serve

1 Mix the flour with 5ml/1 tsp each of salt and black pepper in a shallow dish. Dust the chicken pieces in the flour and set aside.

2 Heat the butter with the oil in a large shallow pan over a medium heat, until the butter is melted. Add the chicken and fry for 5 minutes per side, until golden-brown all over.

3 Add the wine, tomatoes and oregano. Cover the pan and cook for 20–30 minutes, until the chicken is cooked through.

4 Meanwhile, lightly toast the almonds by dry-frying them for 2–3 minutes in a non-stick frying pan. Keep an eye on them as they can burn easily. They should be light golden-brown.

5 Add the almonds to the cooked chicken mixture, season to taste and serve immediately with rice and a crisp green salad.

Cook's tip To joint a chicken, first remove any strings or elastic to release the legs. Using a heavy knife, remove the legs by sliding the knife along the join between the thigh and the body, cutting through the hip joint. Divide the legs into drumsticks and thighs. Next, use a small sharp knife to remove the wishbone from the tail-end of the bird. Discard. Cut along the breastbone from the neck-end to the tail-end, then carefully slice off the breasts. You should now have two thighs, two drumsticks and two breast fillets. Use the carcass to make stock.

Variation This dish is also sometimes served with fried potatoes. Boil 6 large potatoes in their skins until just tender, leave to cool, then peel and slice thickly. Fry in hot oil until golden and crispy on both sides, then sprinkle with salt.

Energy 370kcal/1543kJ; Protein 30g; Carbohydrate 9g, of which sugars 2g; Fat 24g, of which saturates 6g; Cholesterol 121mg; Calcium 53mg; Fibre 2g; Sodium 105mg

Chicken and pea casserole
Pollo arvejado

Simple and quick to make, this one-pot meal is a classic Chilean dish. Most families eat pollo arvejado at least twice a month, and it is especially popular with children.

1 Heat the oil in a large pan. Add the onion and sauté over a medium heat for 8 minutes, then add the garlic and continue to sauté for a further 2 minutes, until the onion is browned. Add the carrot, celery, pepper, oregano, thyme, salt and pepper. Sweat the mixture for about 5 minutes, until tender. Remove from the pan.

2 Add the chicken thighs to the pan with a little extra oil, if needed, and fry for about 5 minutes, on each side, until golden all over. Add the diced potatoes to the pan.

3 Return the sautéed vegetables to the pan. Pour in the wine and enough water to come half way up the chicken pieces. Bring to the boil, cover, and simmer over a low heat for about 30 minutes, until the chicken is tender.

4 Add the peas and cook for 3–4 minutes, adding a little more water if necessary, and seasoning with salt and pepper if needed.

5 Ladle into serving bowls, ensuring everybody has a chicken thigh, and serve.

Serves 6

30ml/2 tbsp olive oil

1 onion, diced

2 cloves garlic, finely chopped

1 carrot, diced

2 celery sticks, diced

½ green (bell) pepper, diced

10ml/2 tsp dried oregano

2 sprigs of fresh thyme

6 large chicken thighs

6 medium potatoes, peeled and diced

50ml/2fl oz/¼ cup white wine

350g/12oz/3 cups fresh or frozen peas

salt and black pepper

Energy 303kcal/1272kJ; Protein 20g; Carbohydrate 35g, of which sugars 5g; Fat 10g, of which saturates 2g; Cholesterol 65mg; Calcium 45mg; Fibre 7g; Sodium 37mg

Stuffed courgettes
Zapallitos rellenos

Serves 4

2 large courgettes (zucchini)

30ml/2 tbsp olive oil

2 garlic cloves, finely chopped

1 onion, peeled and chopped

5ml/1 tsp dried oregano

5ml/1 tsp ground cumin

675g/1½lb/3 cups minced
(ground) beef

2 eggs

60ml/4 tbsp freshly grated
Parmesan cheese

Tomato and Onion Salad (see
page 37), to serve

salt and black pepper

Every Chilean home has its own version of this long-standing family favourite. In this recipe the vegetables are filled with savoury beef and topped with melted cheese.

1 Wash the courgettes and trim off the ends. Place them, whole, in a pan of salted cold water, bring to a simmer and cook for 5–10 minutes, until the flesh is tender but still firm.

2 Remove the courgettes from the pan with a slotted spoon and set aside. When cool enough to handle, cut in half lengthways and use a spoon to remove all the white flesh, reserving it for adding to the meat sauce later. Be careful not to break or split the skin.

3 Preheat the oven to 180°C/350°F/Gas 4. In a large pan, heat the oil over a medium heat.

4 Add the garlic, onion, oregano, cumin, salt and pepper to the pan and fry for 10 minutes, until the onion is softened. Add the beef and cook for about 10 minutes more, stirring, until the meat is browned. Remove from the heat.

5 Mash the courgette flesh with a fork and add it to the pan, then quickly stir in the eggs.

6 Divide the minced beef mixture between the courgettes, and sprinkle the Parmesan cheese on top. Place on a baking sheet and cook in the oven for 15–20 minutes, until the cheese is golden. Serve with Tomato and Onion Salad.

Energy 479kcal/1997kJ; Protein 47g; Carbohydrate 5g, of which sugars 4g; Fat 30g, of which saturates 11g; Cholesterol 223mg; Calcium 171mg; Fibre 1g; Sodium 272mg

Chicken, beef and corn pies
Pastel de choclo

This golden pie is a staple in most Chilean households and a standard feature in restaurants. It combines the filling for empanadas with a crust made from the corn dough used in humitas. It is typically served in individual earthenware bowls. This version has been passed down in my family for generations.

1 Put the chicken thigh fillets in a pan of boiling salted water and simmer for about 20 minutes, until the chicken is cooked through. Remove from the pan and set aside.

2 Meanwhile, make the corn topping. Slice off the kernels by standing the cob upright and carefully slicing down with a sharp knife to remove the kernels. Repeat all round the cob until you have removed all the kernels. Take care not to cut off any of the cob with the kernels, since this is fibrous and tough.

3 Transfer the corn kernels to a food processor and process until the mixture is very fine.

4 Place the lard or white cooking fat for the corn topping in a large pan over a high heat. Once the fat has melted, add the corn paste, basil and salt. Slowly incorporate the milk (a little bit at a time), stirring constantly until the mixture thickens.

5 Add 30ml/2 tbsp sugar to the corn mixture, reduce the heat to low and continue to cook over a low heat for about 5 minutes. Set the mixture aside.

6 Heat 45ml/3 tbsp of the olive oil over a medium heat in a frying pan, then add the onion and garlic and sauté for 10 minutes, until transparent. Add the cumin, paprika and minced beef. Continue to sauté, stirring, for about 5 minutes, until the meat is browned. Stir in the flour, sugar and salt and pepper.

7 Preheat the oven to 200°C/400°F/Gas 6. Using the remaining olive oil, lightly grease the inside of six earthenware bowls, then spread 15ml/1 tbsp of beef filling in the base of each.

8 Cut the hard-boiled eggs into quarters and cut the cooked chicken into six equal parts. Divide the ingredients among the six bowls and arrange one quarter of a hard-boiled egg, a piece of chicken, an olive and 4 raisins on top of the beef mixture in each (you will have half of an egg left over).

9 Cover the filling with the corn topping, spreading it out so that it is even. Sprinkle the tops with the remaining sugar. Bake in the hot oven for 35 minutes, until the crusts are golden-brown. Serve in the earthenware bowls with Tomato and Onion Salad.

Serves 6

500g/1¼lb skinless chicken thigh fillets

1 medium onion, finely chopped

1 garlic clove, finely chopped

90ml/6 tbsp olive oil

5ml/1 tsp ground cumin

10ml/2 tsp paprika

400g/14oz/1¾ cups minced (ground) beef

5ml/1 tsp plain (all-purpose) flour

5ml/1 tsp sugar

2 eggs, hard-boiled and shelled

6 olives, pitted

24 raisins

salt and black pepper

Tomato and Onion Salad (page 37), to serve

For the corn topping

6 large corn on the cob or 1kg/2¼lb frozen corn

45ml/3 tbsp lard or white cooking fat

15 fresh basil leaves, finely torn

5ml/1 tsp salt

475ml/16fl oz/2 cups full-fat (whole) milk

45ml/3 tbsp sugar

Cook's tip Although it is not traditional, you could make the pie in one large earthenware dish.

Energy 610kcal/2259kJ; Protein 44g; Carbohydrate 45g, of which sugars 14g; Fat 29g, of which saturates 11g; Cholesterol 206mg; Calcium 137mg; Fibre 8g; Sodium 874mg

Slow-braised beef
Plateada

Plateada is among the most popular home-cooked dishes in Chile. Slow-cooking the beef draws out the flavour and juices from the meat, which is perfectly complemented by the floury texture and bland taste of bean purée. This is another hearty meal to serve in times of celebration with family and friends.

Serves 6

2kg/4½lb rib cap of beef (see Cook's tip)

60ml/4 tbsp olive oil

4 onions, peeled and quartered

2 carrots, peeled and sliced

1 large ripe tomato, peeled and chopped

2.5ml/½ tsp paprika

250ml/8fl oz/1 cup beef stock

salt and ground black pepper

For the marinade

4 garlic cloves, crushed

5ml/1 tsp salt

15ml/1 tbsp ground black pepper

45ml/3 tbsp olive oil

45ml/3 tbsp red wine vinegar

For the bean purée

2 x 400g cans cannellini or butter (lima) beans

45ml/3 tbsp olive oil

salt and ground black pepper

Cook's tip Plateada literally means 'silver plated', which refers to the silvery skin on the rib side of the meat. The cut is called rib cap in other countries and, while it isn't commonly used outside Chile, should be available in good butchers. It needs long, slow cooking.

1 Place the beef in a shallow dish. Mix together the garlic, salt and pepper for the marinade and rub into the beef. Add the oil and vinegar. Cover and leave to marinate in the refrigerator for 1–2 days, turning the beef over a few times.

2 Bring the meat up to room temperature, then lift it out of the liquid, reserving the marinade, and pat it dry.

3 Heat the oil in a large pan over a medium temperature. Brown the beef for 5 minutes on each side, sealing the meat and giving it a deep colour. Remove from the pan.

4 Add the onion and carrot to the pan and cook for 5–8 minutes; again these should brown well, to add flavour to the dish.

5 Add the tomato, paprika, salt and pepper to the pan, along with the beef stock and the reserved marinade.

6 Replace the meat in the pan. Reduce the heat to low and simmer for 4 hours. Check occasionally and add a little extra water if necessary. Turn off the heat. Lift out the meat on to a carving board, cover with foil and leave to rest for 20 minutes.

7 Meanwhile make the bean purée. Drain and rinse the beans, and place in a pan, with plenty of salt, pepper, the olive oil, and a little water. When the beans are warmed through, mash until smooth with a potato masher. Add a little more water and olive oil, as needed, for a soft consistency.

8 Carve the beef into thick slices, return it to the sauce and reheat very gently. Serve the meat and the juice with bean purée.

Energy 758kcal/3167kJ; Protein 78g; Carbohydrate 26g, of which sugars 10g; Fat 39g, of which saturates 12g; Cholesterol 203mg; Calcium 64mg; Fibre 6g; Sodium 192mg

Simple beef stew
Estofado

Estofado is a basic beef stew cooked with vegetables at a moderately high temperature. Stews are very popular in Chile and this recipe is often eaten on the magical night of San Juan, on 23rd June, when fire festivals mark the summer solstice.

1 Heat the oil in a large pan over a medium heat. Add the steak and cook for 8 minutes or until browned all over.

2 Add the onion to the pan and cook, stirring, for 8 minutes more. Season with salt, pepper, paprika and oregano.

3 Add the carrot, red pepper and potatoes and stir-fry for 5 minutes. Add 350ml/12fl oz/1½ cups water, bring to the boil, then reduce the heat and cook, semi-covered, for 20 minutes.

4 Add more seasoning to taste, then serve hot, sprinkled with chopped parsley.

Serves 4

45ml/3 tbsp vegetable oil

900g/2lb rump (round) steak, cubed

1 onion, sliced

10ml/2 tsp paprika

1.25ml/¼ tsp dried oregano

1 large carrot, sliced

1 large red (bell) pepper, seeded and sliced

4 medium potatoes, peeled and sliced

30ml/2 tbsp chopped fresh parsley, to garnish

salt and black pepper

Energy 610kcal/2554kJ; Protein 55g; Carbohydrate 44g, of which sugars 9g; Fat 25g, of which saturates 7g; Cholesterol 142mg; Calcium 40mg; Fibre 6g; Sodium 170mg

Beef, tomato and corn stew
Tomatican

Serves 4

250g/9oz fillet steak (beef tenderloin)

15ml/1 tbsp vegetable oil

2 onions, finely chopped

15ml/1 tbsp smoked paprika

6 ripe tomatoes

4 corn on the cob

475ml/16fl oz/2 cups of vegetable stock or tomato juice

a pinch of fresh oregano

4 large potatoes, peeled and quartered

salt and black pepper

chopped fresh parsley, to garnish

This Creole-style stew is made from juicy ripe tomatoes, fillet steak and onion, and perfectly showcases the tradition of combining cooking traditions introduced by the Spanish conquistadors with ingredients found in pre-colonial recipes.

1 Cut the steak into 1cm/½in cubes. Heat the oil in a pan over a medium heat, then add the steak and cook for 6 minutes to brown.

2 Add the chopped onions to the pan. Cook for 5 minutes. Add the smoked paprika and stir to mix. Cook for 2 more minutes.

3 Skin the tomatoes by scoring an 'X' at the top of the tomatoes. Immerse them in a bowl of boiling water for 1 minute, then remove to a bowl of cold water and leave for 30 seconds. The skins should now come away easily. Dice the tomatoes.

4 Slice off the kernels from the corn on the cob by slicing downwards with a sharp knife. Add the diced tomatoes, corn kernels and the vegetable stock or tomato juice to the pan. Season with salt, pepper and the oregano.

5 Cover the pan, reduce the heat and cook for 40–50 minutes, until the mixture has thickened. Add more stock or water if required.

6 Place the potatoes in a large pan, cover with water and add salt. Bring to a boil and cook for 20–25 minutes, until tender. Strain and garnish with parsley. Serve the stew with the potatoes.

Energy 462kcal/1952kJ; Protein 25g; Carbohydrate 70g, of which sugars 14g; Fat 11g, of which saturates 3g; Cholesterol 38mg; Calcium 51mg; Fibre 11g; Sodium 297mg

Fries with steak, egg and onion
Chorrillana

A typical dish of Valparaíso and a favourite with young people all over Chile, chorrillana combines French fries with fried onions, steak and scrambled eggs. Said to have originated around 30 years ago in a casino for non-commissioned police officers, it is famously prepared in the restaurant 'J. Cruz'. No trip to this port town would be complete without this ultimate fast-food feast, said to be the perfect hangover cure.

1 Peel the potatoes and slice them into chips (French fries) about 1cm/½in thick.

2 Pour enough oil to come two-thirds of the way up a deep, heavy pan suitable for deep-frying, or in a deep-fat fryer. Heat the oil to 140–160°C/275–325°F. Carefully lower in the chips with a slotted spoon, taking care not to crowd the pan; you may need to cook them in several batches.

3 Fry the chips for 8 minutes, then lift them out on to kitchen paper. Turn the heat down, but keep the oil warm as you will fry the chips for a second time. Be careful when deep-frying as boiling oil is very dangerous.

4 Heat 25ml/1½ tbsp vegetable oil in a frying pan over a medium-high heat, then add the onions and sauté for about 10 minutes, until translucent. Transfer to a dish and set aside.

5 Cut the meat into strips 1cm/½in long. Break the eggs into a large bowl, add a little salt and pepper, and lightly beat with a fork.

6 Heat the remaining 25ml/1½ tbsp oil over a high heat in the frying pan in which you cooked the onions. Add the steak strips and stir-fry for about 3 minutes, until browned all over.

7 Meanwhile, bring the oil for deep-frying up to 160–180°C/325–350°F. Carefully return the chips to the pan using a slotted spoon and fry for 2–3 minutes, until crisp and golden. Lift out with a slotted spoon and drain on kitchen paper. Keep warm.

8 Turn down the heat under the frying pan to medium, add the garlic and cook for 1 minute more. Turn the heat to low, and add the precooked onion, then the beaten eggs, and stir gently to combine and to scramble the egg. Remove from the heat as soon as the egg is just cooked. Take care not to overcook it.

9 To serve the chorrillana, make a mound of fries on each plate, then spoon over some of the meat and egg mixture. Serve immediately with some salsa spooned over the top, or on the side, and a cold beer.

Serves 4

900g/2lb potatoes

50ml/2fl oz/¼ cup vegetable oil, plus extra for deep-frying

2 large onions, peeled and sliced

450g/1lb rump (round) steak, or any cut of your choice

5 eggs

2 garlic cloves, finely chopped

salt and black pepper

Chilean Salsa (see page 36), to serve

Energy 620kcal/2593kJ; Protein 42g; Carbohydrate 48g, of which sugars 8g; Fat 30g, of which saturates 6g; Cholesterol 423mg; Calcium 97mg; Fibre 5g; Sodium 215mg

Meat and fish stew
Pulmay

Pulmay originates from Chiloé Island and is based on the ancient custom of cooking in a pit. Stones are heated in a fire until they are white-hot, then placed in a deep hole. Meat, fish and vegetables are placed on top, with leaves from a local plant dividing the ingredients in layers. Finally everything is covered with hot stones and left for several hours. This recipe is an adaptation that enables the dish to be cooked in a large pot.

Serves 6

6 small chicken pieces

2 garlic cloves, finely chopped

1.25ml/½ tsp dried oregano

4 onions, peeled and cut into thick rings

2 fresh coriander (cilantro) sprigs

2 cabbages, washed and separated into leaves, discarding any tough or brown leaves

3 smoked sausages

6 smoked pork chops

10 small potatoes, washed

1kg/2¼lb mussels, cleaned and 'debearded' (discard any that are not tightly closed)

1kg/2¼lb littleneck clams, cleaned (discard any that are not tightly closed)

3 thick fillets of white fish, such as hake or tilapia

750ml/1¼ pints/3 cups dry white wine

salt and ground black pepper

hot chilli sauce, and Tomato and Onion Salad (see page 37), to serve

Cook's tip Smoked pork chops and sausages can be bought online. If you prefer to use fresh, brown them first in a frying pan on all sides before adding to the pan.

1 In a large bowl, combine the chicken, garlic, oregano and 2.5ml/½ tsp salt. Stir to combine, then cover and marinate for at least 4 hours or overnight in the refrigerator.

2 Place half the onion rings, black pepper and a fresh coriander sprig in the bottom of a deep pan. Cover with a layer of cabbage leaves.

3 Arrange the sausages, chops and marinated chicken on top, then cover with another layer of cabbage leaves.

4 Place the whole washed potatoes in their skins on top, then cover with cabbage leaves. Add the mussels and clams, and another sprig of coriander. Cover with more cabbage leaves and put the fish fillets on top.

5 Cover again with cabbage and the remaining onion rings. Finally cover all the ingredients with the wine. Cover everything with a clean damp dish towel and then the pan lid. Place the pan over a medium heat and simmer for about 1 hour, until the fish is cooked.

6 Put the food on a large serving platter to bring to the table. Discard any mussels or clams that have not opened.

7 Pour the cooking stock into cups or bowls, and serve with the meat and fish. Diners can take a selection of fish, meat and vegetables. Serve with hot chilli sauce and salad.

Energy 510kcal/2148kJ; Protein 71g; Carbohydrate 32g, of which sugars 10g; Fat 12g, of which saturates 3g; Cholesterol 168mg; Calcium 295mg; Fibre 6g; Sodium 965mg

Stuffed potatoes
Papas rellenas

This is a typical dish from the south of Chile, where stuffed potatoes have been part of the culinary heritage of the region for generations. Similar to large croquettes, papas rellenas make a hearty and warming treat for lunch or supper.

1 First, prepare the potato mixture. Wash then peel the potatoes and cut them into small chunks. Place in a large pan of salted boiling water and cook for about 20 minutes, until they are very soft.

2 Drain the potatoes and leave to steam-dry in the strainer for a minute or two. Return to the pan, mash until smooth, then add the milk and butter and stir to combine. Add the egg yolk, flour and salt, and mix just until everything is well combined. Set aside to cool.

3 To make the filling, heat the oil in a frying pan over a medium heat, then add the onion and garlic and sauté for 10 minutes, until soft.

4 Add the paprika, cumin and beef and stir well to break up any large pieces of meat. Add a splash of water, then cook, stirring frequently, for about 10 minutes, until the meat is browned all over. Stir in the raisins, olives and diced egg.

5 Dust your hands with flour, then divide the potato mixture into 10–12 portions. Take one in one hand and make a well in the middle.

6 Fill the well with 15–30ml/1–2 tbsp of the beef mixture. Mould the potato around the beef, adding more if necessary, and shape into a rough oblong with slightly pointy ends. Repeat until all the potato and beef is used up.

7 Heat the oil in a deep frying pan over a high heat until sizzling, then carefully transfer the prepared potato croquettes into the frying pan using a slotted spoon.

8 Fry each batch for 3–4 minutes on each side or until golden all over. You may need to do this in several batches.

9 When cooked, carefully lift out the stuffed potatoes with a slotted spoon and drain on kitchen paper. Serve immediately while they are still warm.

Cook's tip These stuffed potatoes can be made in advance up to the end of step 6, then covered and chilled in the refrigerator until required. When you are ready to cook them, fry for 3 minutes per side, then place in a hot oven for another 8–10 minutes to heat through.

Serves 4–6

4 large potatoes
30ml/2 tbsp milk
30ml/2 tbsp butter
1 egg yolk
50g/2oz/1/2 cup plain (all-purpose) flour
salt, to taste

For the filling

15ml/1 tbsp vegetable oil
1/2 onion, diced
2 garlic cloves, finely chopped
10ml/2 tsp smoked paprika
5ml/1 tsp ground cumin
450g/1lb/2 cups minced (ground) beef
75g/3oz/1/2 cup sultanas (golden raisins)
8 black olives, pitted and sliced
2 hard-boiled eggs, shelled and diced
25g/1oz/1/4 cup plain (all-purpose) flour, for dusting
750ml/1 1/4 pints/3 cups vegetable oil, for frying

Energy 478kcal/1999kJ; Protein 24g; Carbohydrate 43g, of which sugars 11g; Fat 24g, of which saturates 8g; Cholesterol 151mg; Calcium 67mg; Fibre 4g; Sodium 228mg

Patagonian lamb with mashed potatoes

Cordero patagónico con puré rústico

Lamb that has been raised in Patagonia is in the process of becoming recognized with a seal of a geographical indication. The meat stands out from its competitors in terms of flavour and texture due to the grass and wild herbs the sheep graze on. It is showcased perfectly in this roast lamb dish.

1 In a stone mortar, grind the oregano and about 7.5ml/1½ tsp salt with a pestle. Rub this mixture on the surface of the lamb. Set aside.

2 Put the onion, parsley and garlic cloves in the mortar and pound to a purée with the pestle. Transfer to a bowl and add the wine, 175ml/6fl oz/³/₄ cup water and a pinch of salt.

3 Put the lamb in a deep dish, then pour over the marinade, cover the lamb and leave it to marinate for at least 3 hours or overnight.

4 Remove the lamb from the marinade and place in a roasting tray. Reserve the marinade. Smear the lamb with the lard. Allow the lamb to come to room temperature. Preheat the oven to 180°C/350°F/Gas 4.

5 Roast the lamb for about 2½ hours, allowing 25–35 minutes per 450g/1lb, plus an extra 25 minutes, depending on how rare or well-cooked you like your meat.

6 Remove the lamb from the oven, lift it on to a carving dish, cover with foil and leave to rest. Leave the juices in the roasting tray to cool.

7 To make the mashed potatoes, put the potatoes, in their skins, in a large pan and cover with cold salted water. Bring to the boil and simmer for 20–30 minutes, until tender all the way through.

8 Reserve 250ml/8fl oz/1 cup of the cooking water, then drain the potatoes and leave to steam-dry for a couple of minutes. When cool enough to handle, remove the skins. Return the potatoes to the pan and roughly mash them. Add milk and butter and stir to combine.

9 Return the pan to a low heat and add the grated garlic, merquén, cream and plenty of salt and pepper to the potatoes. If the mash is too stiff, add some of the reserved potato water. Stir to combine and heat until piping hot.

10 Skim off any excess fat from the cooled meat juices in the roasting tray, and add the reserved marinade to the tray. Cook the gravy over a low heat, stirring, until reduced.

11 Carve the rested lamb into thick slices and serve on warmed plates with the mashed potatoes and gravy.

Serves 8

15ml/1 tbsp fresh oregano

1.8kg/4lb leg of lamb

1 onion, roughly chopped

10ml/2 tsp finely chopped fresh parsley

4 garlic cloves, roughly chopped

175ml/6fl oz/³/₄ cup white wine

115g/4oz lard or white cooking fat

fresh rosemary, to garnish

For the mashed potatoes

800g/1³/₄lb potatoes, washed and cut into quarters

475ml/16fl oz/2 cups full-fat (whole) milk

115g/4oz/½ cup butter

½ clove garlic, finely grated

5ml/1 tsp merquén (see page 96)

250ml/8fl oz/1 cup double (heavy) cream

salt and black pepper

Energy 775kcal/3219kJ; Protein 44g; Carbohydrate 22g, of which sugars 5g; Fat 57g, of which saturates 29g; Cholesterol 233mg; Calcium 111mg; Fibre 2g; Sodium 230mg

Pork with potatoes
Pernil con papas cocidas

The rearing of pigs and cooking of pork remains deeply traditional in the Chilean countryside. Recipes such as this are most commonly served through the month of September during the Chilean National festivities. The distinct taste of pernil con papas cocidas varies from many other Chilean dishes, but it's a cultural favourite and is served quite simply, with boiled potatoes and salsa.

Serves 4

900g/2lb leg of pork

1 carrot, peeled and sliced

1 onion, peeled and quartered

2 cloves

2 garlic cloves, peeled but left whole

2 bay leaves

1 bouquet garni made from a stick of celery and sprigs of fresh parsley and thyme tied together

8 medium potatoes, washed

salt and black pepper

Chilean Salsa (see page 36), to serve

1 Put the leg of pork in a large pan, together with the carrot, onion, cloves, garlic, bay leaves, bouquet garni and plenty of salt and pepper.

2 Cover with hot water and bring to a boil over a medium heat. Reduce the heat to low, cover the pan and cook for 2–3 hours or until the pork is cooked. If necessary, add more water.

3 Remove from the heat and allow the pork to cool in the cooking liquid overnight.

4 Cook the whole potatoes in a large pan of salted boiling water for 20–30 minutes, until soft and cooked.

5 Meanwhile, place the pan containing the pork back on a medium heat and bring to a gentle boil. Reduce the heat to low, and simmer for about 20 minutes, until the meat is piping hot all the way through.

6 When the potatoes are cooked, drain them and leave to steam. When they are cool enough to handle, peel off the skin. Return the peeled potatoes to the pan and cover to keep warm.

7 Lift out the meat on to a carving board and shred the meat using two forks. Season with salt and pepper. Serve the shredded pork with the whole boiled potatoes and Chilean Salsa. Leftovers are delicious served the next day in sandwiches or wraps.

Energy 363kcal/1529kJ; Protein 37g; Carbohydrate 41g, of which sugars 6g; Fat 7g, of which saturates 2g; Cholesterol 95mg; Calcium 41mg; Fibre 5g; Sodium 126mg

Llama stew with polenta dumplings
Cocido de llama con vegetales y sopones

This dish is typical of northern Chile, and originates from the Diaguita tradition. Recipes from this region typically include the use of meat from llamas and vicuñas, which were herded by the very first nomadic people who inhabited the area. When these nomadic people began to settle they started to cultivate squash, corn, beans and potatoes, and this delicious stew combines all these native ingredients.

1 Heat the lard or white cooking fat in a large pan over a high heat. Add the llama meat portions and fry the meat, turning it occasionally, for about 5 minutes, until sealed and browned all over.

2 Reduce the heat to medium, add the onion and fry for 5 minutes, until softened. Cover with cold water, bring to the boil, cover the pan and simmer over a low heat for 45 minutes.

3 To make the dumplings, place the polenta and a pinch of salt in a large bowl, make a 'well' in the centre, then stir in the egg yolk and about 30ml/2 tbsp water to bind the dough.

4 Take a small amount of the mixture, working it and shaping it into a long oval shape. Set it aside and continue making the dumplings until all the mixture is used.

5 Add the pumpkin, potatoes, green beans, carrots and salt to the stew. Then place the dumplings in the stock. Boil for 25 minutes more, until the vegetables are cooked.

6 Check the seasoning and add more salt if necessary. Serve garnished with parsley.

Variations

- Llama is available online, but you could use lamb or mutton shoulder, or goat, if you prefer.
- The dumplings, or sopones, are very popular in Chilean cuisine and can be prepared with different types of flour, such as wheat flour or quinoa flour.

Serves 4

50g/2oz/¼ cup lard or white cooking fat

450g/1lb llama meat, cut into portions on the bone; do not trim off the fat, as this gives the dish its flavour

1 onion, finely sliced

400g/14oz pumpkin, peeled and diced

4 medium potatoes, peeled and diced

75g/3oz green beans, sliced

2 carrots, finely sliced

a handful of fresh parsley, finely chopped, to garnish

salt

For the dumplings

115g/4oz/1 cup polenta (finely ground cornmeal)

1 egg yolk

Energy 556kcal/2322kJ; Protein 32g; Carbohydrate 58g, of which sugars 9g; Fat 22g, of which saturates 9g; Cholesterol 13mg; Calcium 80mg; Fibre 7g; Sodium 74mg

Rabbit escabeche
Conejo escabechado

Rabbit is one of the healthiest and tastiest meats, being low in fat and high in nutrients. It is enjoyed all over Chile, whether in the countryside or the city, and is available in local markets. The meat is lean, and marinating it before cooking results in optimum flavour and tenderness.

Serves 4

1kg/2¼lb rabbit, cut in quarters (ask your butcher to do this for you)

250ml/8fl oz/1 cup red wine vinegar

5ml/1 tsp fresh oregano

5ml/1 tsp ground cumin

2 cloves

2 bay leaves

90ml/6 tbsp olive oil

2 onions, thickly sliced

2 cloves garlic, finely chopped

1 carrot, peeled and sliced

120ml/4fl oz/½ cup white wine

475ml/16fl oz/2 cups chicken stock

15ml/1 tbsp sugar

200g/7oz/1 cup long grain rice

salt and black pepper

1 Wash the rabbit then place it in a large bowl with 475ml/16fl oz/2 cups cold water, vinegar, oregano, cumin, cloves, bay leaves, salt and pepper. Cover and marinate for a minimum of 6–8 hours, but preferably overnight.

2 Drain the rabbit and discard the marinade. Heat the oil in a large pan over a medium heat, pat dry the rabbit, and add to the pan.

3 Brown the rabbit pieces all over for about 5 minutes, then add the onion, garlic and carrot and cook for 10 minutes, until softened.

4 Add the white wine, chicken stock and sugar, and mix. Cover the pan and leave to simmer for about 40 minutes, until the rabbit is cooked through. Top up with a little water during the cooking time if it looks as though it is dry.

5 Meanwhile, prepare the rice. Rinse the rice thoroughly in a strainer, then place it in a pan with a tight-fitting lid and cover with cold water. Leave it to soak for 20 minutes.

6 Drain off the soaking water and replace with 475ml/16fl oz/2 cups fresh cold water. Bring the water to a simmer with the lid off, then cover and simmer for 8 minutes. Turn off the heat and leave the pan, undisturbed and with the lid on, for 10 minutes, to finish cooking and absorb all the water. Fluff up the rice with a fork just before serving.

7 To serve, place a portion of rice on each warmed plate, then ladle over some of the rabbit pieces and vegetables along with some of the juices.

Energy 593kcal/2483kJ; Protein 32g; Carbohydrate 55g, of which sugars 10g; Fat 29g, of which saturates 6g; Cholesterol 104mg; Calcium 101mg; Fibre 3g; Sodium 356mg

Corn and bean stew
Porotos granados

This bean stew is a delicious meat-free meal. One of Chile's national favourites, it remains true to its Mapuche Indian origins. A simple, economical stew of squash, beans and corn, this is one of the most iconic dishes on the Chilean menu.

1 Heat the oil in a large pan over a medium temperature. Add the onion and sauté for about 10 minutes, until translucent.

2 Add the garlic, paprika, cumin and oregano to the pan and sauté for a further 1–2 minutes. Add the pumpkin and beans, stir and add enough water to cover.

3 Stand the corn on the cob on a board and use a large, sharp knife to slice downwards and remove the corn kernels.

4 Add the corn and basil to the pan and stir to combine. Simmer for 25 minutes, season to taste and serve.

Cook's tip 'Shelling beans' are any type of bean that is popped out of its pod before being eaten. They can either be eaten fresh, as in this recipe, or dried and stored. Examples include cannellini, butter (wax) or haricot (navy) beans. If you are unable to buy fresh shelling beans, simply use 600g/1lb 6oz soaked, cooked dried beans or canned beans instead.

Serves 6

45ml/3 tbsp vegetable oil

1 onion, chopped

3 garlic cloves, finely chopped

5ml/1 tsp paprika

5ml/1 tsp ground cumin

5ml/1 tsp dried oregano

450g/1lb pumpkin, peeled and diced

2kg/4½lb fresh shelling beans (see Cook's tip)

3 corn on the cob

6 fresh basil leaves, chopped

salt and black pepper

Energy 234kcal/982kJ; Protein 12g; Carbohydrate 25g, of which sugars 6g; Fat 10g, of which saturates 1g; Cholesterol 0mg; Calcium 60mg; Fibre 10g; Sodium 35mg

Wheat berry risotto with beef jerky and fried potatoes

Guiso de mote con charqui y papas doradas

Serves 8

400g/14oz/2 cups wheat berries, soaked in cold water overnight

475ml/16fl oz/2 cups full-fat (whole) milk

475ml/16fl oz/2 cups double (heavy) cream

50g/2oz/^{2}/$_3$ cup grated Parmesan cheese

115g/4oz/1 cup grated mozzarella cheese

25g/1oz/1 tbsp butter

For the beef jerky

30ml/2 tbsp olive oil

^{1}/$_2$ onion, sliced

250g/9oz/1^1/$_2$ cups dried beef jerky, shredded

For the fried potatoes

500ml/17fl oz/generous 2 cups vegetable oil

8 potatoes, peeled and cut into slices 1cm/^{1}/$_2$in thick

salt and black pepper

Wheat berries are an Andean cereal that contain a high level of carbohydrates, fibre and antioxidants. This recipe combines them with two other ingredients that are the basis of many Chilean recipes: potatoes and dried beef jerky.

1 To make the jerky mixture, heat the oil in a frying pan over a medium heat, then add the onion and cook for 7 minutes or until soft. Add the jerky and cook for 3 minutes. Set aside.

2 Drain the wheat berries. Put the milk and the wheat berries in a large pan, cover, place on a low heat and cook for 50 minutes, stirring from time to time.

3 Now make the deep-fried potatoes. Heat the oil in a deep pan over a medium heat to 180°C/350°F. Add half the potatoes to the pan and fry for 10 minutes, until crisp and golden. Remove the potatoes from the oil and drain. Repeat with the rest of the potatoes.

4 Add the cream, grated cheeses and butter to the wheat berry risotto and cook for 1 minute more. Season to taste with salt and pepper, then remove from the heat. Divide the potatoes between shallow serving dishes, then cover each with a layer of risotto. Sprinkle over the jerky mixture and serve immediately.

Cook's tip Wheat berries are hulled wheat kernels, and are packed with nutrients. They are available as either a hard or a soft processed grain, and are reddish-brown in colour. They make a nutritious alternative to rice or corn and are cooked in much the same way as pearl barley. They are often available in health food stores and larger supermarkets.

Energy 786kcal/3269kJ; Protein 25g; Carbohydrate 44g, of which sugars 4g; Fat 58g, of which saturates 30g; Cholesterol 126mg; Calcium 252mg; Fibre 3g; Sodium 870mg

Bean purée bake
Puré de porotos gratinados al merquén

Bean dishes are an important part of the daily diet in Chile, often eaten in the south of the country. This one is spiced with merquén, a traditional seasoning of the native Mapuche people, made from smoked chillies with salt and coriander seeds. This sustaining bake makes a complete vegetarian main meal but can also be served as an accompaniment to roasted meat on a cold winter's day.

1 Soak the beans overnight in a bowl of cold water. Drain, then place the beans in a large pan and cover with fresh water. Bring to the boil and cook for 1½–2 hours, until tender.

2 In a separate large pan, heat the oil over a medium heat and add the onion. Cook for about 6 minutes, until the onion is translucent. Add the paprika and the cooked beans, the butter and the rest of the oil, stir, then cook over a low-medium heat for 4 minutes more.

3 Transfer the mixture to a food processor or use a stick blender to process briefly to a purée. Add the cream and season to taste with salt, pepper and hot pepper sauce and stir. Preheat the oven to 180°C/350°F/Gas 4.

4 Return the mixture to the pan if necessary and cook for 5 minutes more, until hot.

5 Spread half the bean mixture in a baking dish. Distribute half of the Cheddar over the top, then cover with the rest of the beans.

6 Cover the top with the remaining Cheddar cheese, Parmesan cheese and merquén. Cook in the oven for 15 minutes or until golden brown. Serve hot or warm, with salad and bread.

Cook's tip If you can't find any merquén, make your own with equal quantities of Spanish smoked paprika, coriander seeds, dry roasted then ground, and some dried chilli flakes. Mix, and store in an airtight container.

Serves 6–8

700g/1lb 9oz/2 cups dried white beans, such as cannellini beans

45ml/3 tbsp olive oil

1 onion, finely chopped

5ml/1 tsp paprika

50g/2oz/2 tbsp butter

250ml/8fl oz/1 cup double (heavy) cream

15ml/1 tbsp hot pepper sauce

300g/11oz mild Cheddar cheese, grated

25g/1oz Parmesan cheese, grated

10ml/2 tsp merquén, to sprinkle

salt and black pepper

crisp green salad, and crusty bread, to serve

Energy 686kcal/2863kJ; Protein 28g; Carbohydrate 49g, of which sugars 5g; Fat 43g, of which saturates 24g; Cholesterol 95mg; Calcium 407mg; Fibre 17g; Sodium 404mg

Chilean steamed corn cakes
Humitas

A traditional recipe passed down through many generations, humitas are similar to Mexican tamales, and are eaten in vast quantities all over Chile. They are made from fresh corn, which is ground and mixed with salt and lard and then wrapped in corn husks and steamed. They are delicious, and fun to make.

Serves 8

12 large corn on the cob, with husks

30ml/2 tbsp lard or white cooking fat

1 large onion, finely chopped

1 green chilli, deseeded and chopped

a bunch of fresh basil, finely chopped

15ml/1 tbsp paprika

250ml/8fl oz/1 cup full-fat (whole) milk

salt and black pepper

Tomato and Onion Salad (see page 37) to serve

1 Cut the ends off of the corn on the cob, then carefully remove the layers of husk, reserving the widest ones in pairs to make the wrappers for the tamales.

2 Slice the corn from the cob with a sharp knife, standing the cob up on a board and cutting downwards. Grind the kernels in a blender, until a smooth paste forms.

3 Melt the lard or white cooking fat in a frying pan over a medium heat. Add the onion, green chilli, basil, paprika, salt and pepper and sauté for about 10 minutes, until soft and fragrant.

4 Add the puréed corn to the sautéed onion mixture. Add the milk and mix well to form a thick mixture.

5 Place the corn husks in a pan of boiling water for a couple of minutes to soften them. Slice one of the husks into thin strips for tying.

6 Working in a shallow baking tray to catch any excess mixture that may spill, place two husks side by side, overlapping them at their widest part. Place 45ml/3 tbsp of the corn mixture on the wide part of the husk, fold the leaves in from the sides then fold in the ends to form a neat parcel.

7 Tie around the middle to secure with the thin strip of husk. Prepare the others in the same way, until all of the mixture is used.

8 Place the tamales in a large pan of salted boiling water and simmer for 1 hour. Carefully lift out the tamales using a slotted spoon, leave to cool slightly and then serve in their wrappers. Each person unwraps their tamale to eat the corn filling, with Tomato and Onion Salad.

Energy 258kcal/1081kJ; Protein 7g; Carbohydrate 35g, of which sugars 4g; Fat 11g, of which saturates 3g; Cholesterol 51mg; Calcium 30mg; Fibre 4g; Sodium 168mg

Sweet Things

Many of the desserts made at home in Chile are based on milk and fruit, while baked treats are often bought at a local pâtisserie and taken home, or presented as a gift when visiting friends.

Baked milk pudding
Leche asada

Although this dish consists of a simple combination of a few ingredients, it makes a most delicious dessert. Most South American cuisines have their own version of this Spanish milk pudding. The Chilean version is accompanied by a rich caramel, which adds a special touch to both the taste and the appearance. Leche asada is a much-loved favourite throughout the country.

1 Preheat the oven to 180°C/350°F/Gas 4. To make the caramel, place the sugar and lemon juice in a heavy pan, with 90ml/6 tbsp cold water, and cook over a medium heat, without stirring, until the sugar has all dissolved.

2 Reduce the heat a little and continue to simmer until the caramel reaches the hard-crack stage, or 168°C/336°F on a sugar thermometer. You can also judge the mixture by eye; you are looking for a dark golden-brown colour. Take care with boiling sugar as it is dangerous, and do not let the mixture burn or it will be bitter and inedible.

3 At the point of caramelization, quickly remove the pan from the heat and pour the caramel into a 3.6 litre/6 pint/15 cup baking dish.

4 Beat the eggs in a large bowl. Add the milk, cloves, cinnamon, vanilla and sugar and beat together until well combined.

5 Pour the custard mixture into the baking dish over the caramel.

6 Bake in the oven for about 30 minutes, until the custard is set but still has a slight wobble, and the top is golden brown.

7 Cool the pudding to room temperature, then refrigerate for 5–8 hours. Serve cold, spooned into dessert bowls, flipped with caramel on top.

Serves 8

For the caramel sauce

200g/7oz/1 cup white sugar

5 drops of lemon juice

For the milk mixture

6 eggs

1 litre/1³/₄ pints/4 cups full-fat (whole) milk

5 cloves

1 cinnamon stick

the scraped seeds from one vanilla pod (bean), or 5ml/1 tsp vanilla extract

90ml/6 tbsp white sugar

Energy 291kcal/1224kJ; Protein 10g; Carbohydrate 44g, of which sugars 44g; Fat 10g, of which saturates 4g; Cholesterol 196mg; Calcium 117mg; Fibre 0g; Sodium 120mg

Honey pudding with marrons glacés

Budín de miel de palma con castañas confitadas

The National Park La Campana in the Valparaíso region is the country's largest reserve of Chilean palm trees. The much-loved syrup produced from the sap of these trees is called honey by Chileans, and it gives a special flavour to drinks and desserts. Luxurious marrons glacés are chestnuts that are preserved in syrup and then candied; they are popular at Christmas, but are available throughout the year online.

Serves 8

90g/3½oz/½ cup white sugar

375g/13oz/1 cup palm honey

250ml/8 fl oz/1 cup full-fat (whole) milk

200g/7oz sponge cake, crumbled

grated rind of 1 lemon

2.5ml/½ tsp ground cinnamon

120ml/4fl oz/½ cup dark rum

60ml/4 tbsp butter, melted, plus extra for greasing

4 eggs, whites and yolks separated

250ml/8fl oz/1 cup whipping cream

250g/9oz/2 cups marrons glacés (glazed chestnuts) in syrup

Cook's tip If you can't find palm honey, substitute maple syrup or a strongly-flavoured honey such as manuka.

1 Preheat the oven to 180°C/350°F/Gas 4. Place the sugar and 45ml/3 tbsp cold water in a pan and cook over a medium heat, without stirring, until it forms a caramel, then immediately remove from the heat.

2 Wearing oven gloves add 275g/10oz/¾ cup palm honey, and then the milk, stirring until well blended. The caramel may bubble and spit when you add the liquids, so take great care.

3 Put the crumbled sponge cake, lemon rind, cinnamon, rum and melted butter in a bowl. Mix well to combine.

4 Beat the egg whites until stiff in a different bowl. In a third bowl, beat the egg yolks until frothy. Alternately add the egg white and egg yolks to the cake mixture, until combined.

5 Lightly butter 8 individual pudding moulds or ramekins and divide the mixture between them. Place the moulds in a deep baking tray and carefully pour in boiling water to come halfway up the sides of the moulds.

6 Bake for 8–10 minutes, until set and golden-brown. Remove from the oven, take out of the water bath and set aside for 10 minutes. Run a knife around the sides of the moulds to release the puddings, then upturn each on to an individual dessert plate. Drizzle with the remaining honey.

7 Serve warm or cold, topped with whipped cream and a glazed chestnut.

Energy 319kcal/1335kJ; Protein 7g; Carbohydrate 35g, of which sugars 26g; Fat 18g, of which saturates 7g; Cholesterol 167mg; Calcium 80mg; Fibre 1g; Sodium 185mg

Snow milk
Leche nevada

Serves 4

3 eggs

165g/5½oz/generous ¾ cup caster (superfine) sugar

750ml/1¼ pints/3 cups full-fat (whole) milk

5ml/1 tsp vanilla extract

10ml/2 tsp cornflour (cornstarch)

ground cinnamon, for dusting

This classic Chilean dessert is served cold and is really delicious. It owes its name to the little pillows of soft meringue, which resemble snow, that are placed on the lightly-set custard mixture, or 'cooked milk', as the Chileans call it.

1 First separate the eggs, putting the whites in a large, grease-free bowl and the yolks in a small bowl. Beat the whites until stiff peaks form, then beat in 15ml/1 tbsp of the sugar. Set the meringue aside.

2 Put the milk, the remaining sugar and the vanilla extract in a pan and bring to a simmer over a low heat. Using two spoons, place little mounds of meringue into the simmering milk, and cook for 2 minutes, turning once.

3 When the meringues are firm, lift out of the milk with a slotted spoon.

4 Transfer the meringues to a large dish with a lid, in which they can rest in a single layer.

5 Dissolve the cornflour in 15ml/1 tbsp cold water, then whisk in the paste, along with the egg yolks, to the milk and sugar mixture in the pan. Stir continuously over a low heat until it is thick enough to coat the back of a spoon. Remove from the heat.

6 Pour the custard into dishes, cover with clear film (plastic wrap), and chill for at least 3 hours. To serve, carefully position several meringues on top of each custard and sprinkle with cinnamon.

Energy 361kcal/1517kJ; Protein 12g; Carbohydrate 54g, of which sugars 52g; Fat 12g, of which saturates 6g; Cholesterol 205mg; Calcium 251mg; Fibre 0g; Sodium 148mg

Red wine meringue mousse
Turrón de vino

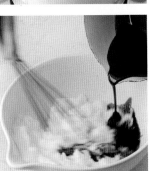

Chile produces excellent wines, so why not make a dessert with one of them? Turrón de vino is a popular treat that was created in colonial times, and is often served to guests during the Christmas holidays at the end of a large meal.

1 Combine the sugar, the lemon juice and the wine in a pan over a medium heat and bring to a boil, stirring to dissolve the sugar. Boil until the mixture has reduced by half, and a thick syrup has formed.

2 Meanwhile, in a grease-free bowl, beat the egg whites until stiff peaks have formed.

3 Gradually add the hot syrup to the egg whites, slowly trickling it down the side of the bowl and beating well constantly. Keep beating until the meringue is very firm.

4 Scoop spoonfuls of the mousse into glasses and decorate with the toasted chopped nuts. Refrigerate for at least 2 hours, then serve.

Serves 6

250g/9oz/1½ cups caster (superfine) sugar

6 drops of lemon juice

175ml/6fl oz/¾ cup red wine

3 egg whites

150g/5oz/1 cup chopped nuts, to decorate

Energy 342kcal/1436kJ; Protein 7g; Carbohydrate 46g, of which sugars 45g; Fat 14g, of which saturates 2g; Cholesterol 0mg; Calcium 27mg; Fibre 2g; Sodium 110mg

Fruit syrup ice cream
Helado de chañar

The chañar tree bears fruit that is the same size and shape of an olive. It can be eaten fresh, or made into jellies or prepared liquors. Chañar fruit was an important part of the diet of the first inhabitants of the Atacama. Chañar syrup is quite difficult to find outside Chile, but you can replace it with your favourite fruit syrup: pomegranate, fig or raspberry syrups would all work well in this recipe.

1 Put the cream in a large bowl and whip with an electric or balloon whisk until soft peaks form. Place the bowl in the refrigerator.

2 Put the milk, sugar and egg yolks in a heavy pan and heat gently over a low heat, stirring constantly, until it reaches a temperature of 82°C/180°F and a smooth custard forms, thick enough to coat the back of a spoon.

3 Transfer the custard to a large bowl and cover the surface with a piece of clear film (plastic wrap) or dust with icing (confectioners') sugar, to prevent a skin from forming. Leave to cool to room temperature.

Serves 4

250ml/8fl oz/1 cup whipping cream

250ml/8fl oz/1 cup full-fat (whole) milk

75ml/5 tbsp caster (superfine) sugar

2 egg yolks

50ml/2fl oz/¼ cup chañar or other fruit syrup, plus extra, for trickling

berry compôte, to serve

4 Add the chañar, or fruit syrup and the whipped cream to the custard, and fold them in to combine thoroughly. Transfer to a plastic container and freeze for 6 hours.

5 Stir the mixture every hour to prevent ice crystals from forming. Alternatively you can churn the mixture in an ice cream machine.

6 Remove the ice cream from the freezer around 20 minutes before you wish to serve it to allow it to soften slightly.

7 Place two scoops of ice cream on each of four dessert plates, add a spoonful of berry compôte and trickle over some extra syrup.

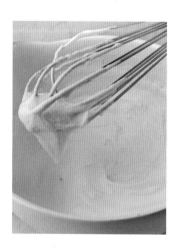

Energy 413kcal/1716kJ; Protein 5g; Carbohydrate 32g, of which sugars 32g; Fat 30g, of which saturates 18g; Cholesterol 175mg; Calcium 124mg; Fibre 0g; Sodium 83mg

Papaya tart
Pastel relleno con papayas

This delectable dessert originates from the cuisine of the Diaguita Andean people who inhabited the north of Chile. The pastry is made from ground quinoa flour, and so combines two ingredients that are typical of the region: papaya and quinoa.

Serves 4

For the pastry

225g/8oz/2 cup quinoa flour

115g/4oz/½ cup butter, at room temperature

50g/2oz/¼ cup caster (superfine) sugar

For the filling

250ml/8fl oz/1 cup full-fat (whole) milk

25g/1oz/¼ cup cornflour (cornstarch)

1 egg yolk

25g/1oz/2 tbsp caster (superfine) sugar

2 ripe papaya or 225g/8oz canned papaya, drained

Cook's tip Quinoa flour can be bought in health stores or online, but you can also make your own by blitzing uncooked white quinoa in a food processor.

1 First, make the pastry. Sift the flour into a bowl and mix with the butter, then add the sugar. Knead briefly until a homogenous dough forms, then shape into a ball, wrap in clear film (plastic wrap) and refrigerate for 30 minutes.

2 Roll out the dough to a circle large enough to line a 15cm/6in pie tin (pan). Pastry made with quinoa flour can be quite fragile, if so, simply press the dough into the pan with your fingertips. Then chill for a further 20 minutes. Preheat the oven to 180°C/350°F/Gas 4.

3 Prick the pastry lightly with a fork and line with baking parchment and baking beans. Bake the pastry for 15 minutes, then remove the paper and return to the oven to cook for a further 5 minutes, until the pastry is light golden in colour.

4 Meanwhile, prepare the filling. Put 120ml/4fl oz/½ cup of the milk in a bowl with the cornflour and egg yolk and stir to create a smooth paste.

5 Combine the rest of the milk with the sugar in a pan. Bring to a boil over a medium heat, then add the milk and cornflour paste and stir to combine. Bring to the boil then cook, stirring constantly, for 1 minute more.

6 Remove the pan from the heat and cover with a lid to prevent a skin from forming while the custard mixture cools. Peel the papaya and cut the flesh into uniform slices.

7 Fill the pastry case with the custard and arrange the papayas decoratively on top. Refrigerate for 1 hour before serving.

Energy 475kcal/1986kJ; Protein 7g; Carbohydrate 49g, of which sugars 29g; Fat 29g, of which saturates 17g; Cholesterol 120mg; Calcium 123mg; Fibre 2g; Sodium 228mg

Cookie twists
Calzones rotos

Pastry twists are a favourite Chilean teatime snack. Calzones rotos literally means 'torn trousers', a name which comes from the shape, formed by passing one end of a strip of dough through a slit in the other, forming a loop.

1 Sift the flour, baking powder and sugar in a pile on a work surface. Make a well in the centre and add the butter, egg, egg yolks, lemon rind and brandy. Mix together with your hands, gradually adding 200ml/7fl oz/1 cup cold water, to form a soft dough. Do not knead.

2 On the same surface, roll out the dough until it is 5mm/¼in thick. Add flour as necessary.

3 Using a sharp knife, cut 3cm/1¼in wide strips and then cut these strips on the diagonal to form diamonds 5cm/2in long.

4 Cut a small slit in the middle of each diamond. Pass one end of the diamond through the slit and turn it to form a pastry twist.

5 Two-thirds fill a deep, heavy pan suitable for deep-frying with vegetable oil. Heat the oil over a medium heat until it reaches 190°C/375°F.

6 Lower a few twists into the pan with a slotted spoon, taking care not to crowd them. Fry for 2–3 minutes, until golden. Remove with a slotted spoon and repeat until you have cooked all the twists. Serve dusted with icing sugar.

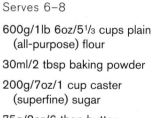

Serves 6–8

600g/1lb 6oz/5⅓ cups plain (all-purpose) flour

30ml/2 tbsp baking powder

200g/7oz/1 cup caster (superfine) sugar

75g/3oz/6 tbsp butter, softened

1 egg, plus 2 egg yolks

15ml/1 tbsp grated lemon rind

30ml/2 tbsp brandy

vegetable oil, for deep frying

icing (confectioners') sugar, for dusting

Energy 498kcal/2102kJ; Protein 9g; Carbohydrate 86g, of which sugars 27g; Fat 15g, of which saturates 6g; Cholesterol 100mg; Calcium 162mg; Fibre 3g; Sodium 516mg

Banana cake
Poe de plátano

Serves 12

1.3kg/3lb ripe bananas

1kg/2¼lb pumpkin, peeled and coarsely grated

675g/1½lb/6 cups plain (all-purpose) flour, sifted

600ml/1 pint/2½ cups vegetable oil, plus extra for greasing

450g/15oz/3 cups grated fresh coconut

400g/14oz/3½ cups white sugar

This delectable and unique cake comes from Easter Island, where you can find more than 15 different types of banana, varying in size and taste. Bananas are eaten on this remote island during most meals as a vegetable accompaniment.

1 Preheat the oven to 180°C/350°F/Gas 4. Squish the bananas with your hand in a large bowl. Add the grated pumpkin and half the flour and mix with your hands to combine.

2 Add the oil and the remaining flour to the bowl, with 350g/12oz/2¼ cups of the grated coconut and the sugar. Mix to form a dough.

3 Lightly grease a 15cm/6in cake tin (pan) and line with baking parchment. Pour in the mixture and cook for 30 minutes, until the cake is golden brown and a skewer inserted in the middle comes out clean. Remove from the oven and leave to cool in the tin.

4 Once the cake is cold, remove from the tin, discard the paper and turn out the cake on to a serving plate. Garnish with the remaining grated coconut and serve in slices.

Cook's tip To prepare fresh coconut: first, drain the coconut water by puncturing two holes through the dark spot on the shell of the coconut, with a clean screwdriver. Reserve the water for drinking. Next, place the coconut on a dampened cloth, to stop it from slipping, on a hard surface. Bang the coconut with a hammer until a crack appears, then prise open the coconut with the screwdriver. Cut out the white flesh, using a strong knife.

Energy 982kcal/4100kJ; Protein 8g; Carbohydrate 99g, of which sugars 54g; Fat 65g, of which saturates 18g; Cholesterol 0mg; Calcium 115mg; Fibre 9g; Sodium 11mg

Iquique cookie sandwiches
Chumbeque

The story goes that this recipe was created by a Chinese immigrant who married a Chilean sweet-maker. Remembering a Chinese man called Chung, who had made a similar confection, the immigrant dubbed the dish 'el queque de Chung', which means 'the cake of Chung'. This was then shortened to chumbeque. The sweet is very popular in the northern city Iquique, and is loved by students for its high calorie content.

1 In a bowl mix the sifted flour, bicarbonate of soda and the salt. Add the melted lard or white cooking fat and mix to combine, until the mixture resembles breadcrumbs.

2 Add 120ml/4fl oz/½ cup cold water and egg yolks to the bowl, stir to combine then tip on to a floured surface. Knead to form a soft dough. Preheat the oven to 180°C/350°F/Gas 4.

3 Cut the dough into three equal parts and roll out with a rolling pin into very thin, long strips. Cut these into 8 equal-sized rectangles, like thin shortbreads. Prick the dough rectangles with a fork and put them on baking sheets. Bake for 20 minutes, until golden-brown.

4 In a pan, mix the honey with the sugar, lemon juice and rind, cinnamon stick and fig leaves. Stir over a medium heat until the sugar has dissolved, then simmer for about 10 minutes until the mixture is a light golden colour.

5 Remove the rind, cinnamon stick and fig leaves from the pan and discard.

6 On a large baking sheet, lined with baking parchment, place a third of the pastry squares. Making sure the syrup is still hot, use a spoon to drizzle a third of the hot honey and sugar mixture over the squares.

7 Carefully top each honey-topped base with another pastry square, and then cover the surface of these with another third of the honey and sugar mixture. Finish each sandwich with another pastry square and honey topping. Press down gently and leave to cool before serving.

8 The sandwiches can be stored in an airtight container at room temperature for up to two weeks.

Variation Several versions of this confection are available in bakeries and stores in Chile, including chocolate, mango and orange flavours. To make orange- or mango-flavoured chumbeque, simply substitute the lemon rind and juice in the syrup mixture with the same quantity of orange rind and juice, or mango syrup.

Serves 8

400g/14oz/3½ cups plain (all-purpose) flour, sifted

15ml/1 tbsp bicarbonate of soda (baking soda)

2.5ml/½ tsp salt

225g/8oz/1 cup lard or white cooking fat, melted

6 egg yolks

90ml/6 tbsp honey

690g/17½oz/3½ cups white sugar

juice and rind of 1 lemon

1 cinnamon stick

2 fig leaves in brine, rinsed

   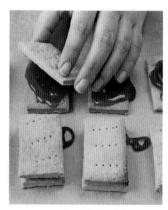

Energy 1119kcal/4711kJ; Protein 9g; Carbohydrate 184g, of which sugars 133g; Fat 43g, of which saturates 17g; Cholesterol 236mg; Calcium 130mg; Fibre 2g; Sodium 731mg

Figs stuffed with almonds
Higos rellenos con almendras

Fig crops in Chile are prolific, and international markets are starting to make use of them and export the high quality fruit all over the world. Closer to home, local figs are enjoyed throughout their season, and this wonderful, simple dessert is sure to delight the palate as well as providing a feast for the eyes.

Serves 4

50g/2oz/¹/₂ cup blanched almonds

50g/2oz/¹/₄ cup dried apricots

30ml/2 tbsp soft light brown sugar

5ml/1 tsp honey

2.5/¹/₂ tsp ground cinnamon

350ml/12fl oz/1¹/₂ cups orange juice

90g/3¹/₂oz/¹/₂ cup caster (superfine) sugar

30ml/2 tbsp dry white wine

1 cinnamon stick

12 fresh figs

vanilla ice cream or double (heavy) cream, to serve (optional)

Variation If pressed for time you could substitute 50g/2oz/¹/₂ cup ground almonds for the blanched almonds and skip steps 1 and 2. However toasting fresh nuts gives a much better depth of flavour.

1 Preheat the oven to 180°C/350°F/Gas 4. Place the blanched almonds on a baking sheet and toast them in the oven for 6–8 minutes or until they turn golden brown. Keep a close eye on them as they burn easily. Keep the oven on.

2 Cool the nuts, grind in a food processor, then transfer to a bowl.

3 Chop the apricots into small pieces and mix with the ground almonds. Add the sugar, honey and ground cinnamon.

4 Mix the almond mixture with your hands until smooth, and make 12 equal-sized balls the size of a walnut.

5 Put the orange juice, caster sugar, wine and the cinnamon stick in a pan and stir to combine and to dissolve the sugar. Cook over a medium heat for about 5 minutes, until a syrup forms. Remove from the heat and leave to cool.

6 Wash the figs and trim the tops. Carefully cut a deep cross in the top, making sure you don't cut all the way to the bottom.

7 Place one almond ball inside each fig, and put them on a greased baking tray.

8 Pour the orange and white wine syrup over the figs. Cook in the oven, at 180°C/350°F/Gas 4, for 10–15 minutes, until the figs are tender and the nut paste has softened and begun to caramelize.

9 Remove the figs from the oven and leave to cool slightly. Serve the figs and their syrup warm, accompanied by a scoop of vanilla ice cream or cream if you like.

Energy 318kcal/1349kJ; Protein 6g; Carbohydrate 61g, of which sugars 61g; Fat 8g, of which saturates 1g; Cholesterol 0mg; Calcium 117mg; Fibre 8g; Sodium 21mg

Squash preserve with nuts
Dulce de alcayota con nueces

The spaghetti squash has been cultivated in America for centuries and is often preserved as a kind of jam. This uniquely Chilean preserve is not only used for spreading on bread, but is also eaten on its own as a dessert or as a filling for sweet empanadas. Preparing this unusual sweet treat at home is very satisfying.

1 Preheat the oven to 200°C/400°F/Gas 6. Bake the whole squash for 2 hours, turning every 20 minutes, until it is soft. Leave to cool.

2 Split the squash and remove the seeds. Remove the soft flesh and place this in a bowl. Add the sugar to the bowl and stir well. Leave it to stand for 12 hours. This is important for the texture of the fruit in the preserve.

3 The next day, transfer the mixture to a heavy pan and simmer gently over a low heat for 20 minutes, stirring frequently.

4 Stir in the orange rind and cloves, then simmer for 25 minutes more. Meanwhile, put a plate or saucer in the freezer.

5 To test whether the jam is ready, place a small amount on the cold plate or saucer, leave it for a few seconds and then push it from the edge with your finger. A skin should have formed on the surface of the jam, and this should wrinkle when you push the jam. This is called the 'wrinkle test'. If the jam does not wrinkle, keep cooking it until it does.

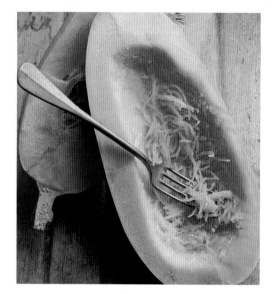

6 Spoon the hot jam into hot sterilized jars (see Cook's tip), then leave to cool, label and store in the refrigerator.

7 Toast the walnuts in a low oven until crisp. Keep a close eye on these, as they easily scorch. Allow to cool, then roughly chop. Serve the preserve on fresh bread, with the toasted walnuts, or with thin slices of cheese and a glass of sweet wine, as a classic dessert.

Serves 8

1 spaghetti squash

675g/1 ½lb/3½ cups white sugar

rind of 1 orange

3 cloves

50g/2oz/½ cup walnuts, chopped

Cook's tip You should always sterilize the jars when making preserves. You can either put them on the top shelf of a dishwasher and run a hot wash, or you can wash them by hand, place them on a baking sheet and put them in a cold oven. Set the oven to 140°C/275°F/Gas 1 and then leave the jars for about 25 minutes. Do not place the cold jars in a preheated oven or they may crack.

Energy 392kcal/1664kJ; Protein 1g; Carbohydrate 92g, of which sugars 91g; Fat 5g, of which saturates 0g; Cholesterol 0mg; Calcium 29mg; Fibre 2g; Sodium 15mg

Drinks

Chilean wine or pisco sours are not the only popular drinks. Fruit punches and liqueurs are also enjoyed in city and village bars, and in back yards for the family barbecues at weekends.

Dried peaches and wheat berries
Mote con huesillos

This delicious, refreshing non-alcoholic drink is found in many parts of the country. It is prepared and enjoyed by people of all ages, from the start of spring and through the summer, and is sold on the streets, in every square and on every beach.

1 Place the peaches and soaking liquid in a pan. Add the soft dark brown sugar, bring to the boil and cook for 45 minutes. Add the white sugar and cinnamon, then continue cooking for 30 minutes or until the peaches are tender.

2 Remove the pan from the heat and leave the peaches to cool in the liquid.

3 Place the wheat berries in a separate pan, cover with cold water and cook over a medium heat for 25 minutes. Drain and rinse.

4 Place 30ml/2 tbsp of the wheat berries in each glass, top with a cooked peach, and then fill to the top with the cooking liquid from the peaches. Serve cold.

Serves 6

250g/9oz/generous 1 cup dried peaches, soaked in 1 litre/1³/₄ pints/4 cups cold water overnight

30ml/2 tbsp soft dark brown sugar

90g/3¹/₂oz/¹/₂ cup white sugar

1 cinnamon stick

250g/9oz/generous 1 cup wheat berries, soaked in 1 litre/1³/₄ pints/4 cups cold water overnight, then drained

Energy 317kcal/1350kJ; Protein 7g; Carbohydrate 68g, of which sugars 38g; Fat 4g, of which saturates 0g; Cholesterol 0mg; Calcium 42mg; Fibre 8g; Sodium 17mg

Pisco sour with basil and green chilli
Pisco sour con albahaca y ají verde

Serves 4

ice cubes

100ml/3½fl oz/scant ½ cup pisco

30ml/2 tbsp lemon juice

50ml/2fl oz/¼ cup egg white

50ml/2fl oz/¼ cup sugar syrup

10 fresh basil leaves, chopped, plus whole leaves to garnish

½ green chilli, deseeded and finely chopped

4 thin slices of lemon, to garnish

The Elqui Valley has 300 days of sunshine per year, and the area provides the perfect climate for the grape that, after a long, traditional process, results in this unique brandy. In Chile, pisco is the base for over 60 aperitifs and cocktails.

1 Place a few ice cubes, the pisco, lemon juice, egg white, sugar syrup, fresh basil and chopped green chilli in a cocktail shaker. Shake vigorously for 30–45 seconds.

2 Strain the mixture straight into chilled champagne flutes, garnish the glass with a slice of lemon and a basil leaf and serve straight away.

Energy 73kcal/311kJ; Protein 2g; Carbohydrate 13g, of which sugars 13g; Fat 0g, of which saturates 0g; Cholesterol 0mg; Calcium 8mg; Fibre 0g; Sodium 26mg

Cherry liqueur
Enguindado

Serves 8

1kg/2¼lb cherries

500ml/17fl oz/generous 2 cups brandy

400g/14oz/2 cups white sugar

This homemade liqueur is often made as a way to preserve cherries when they ripen all at once on the trees and need to be eaten. It is ideal for serving as a digestif after a good dinner, and also makes a perfect Christmas tipple.

1 Wash the cherries, then remove the pits and cut the cherries in half. Place the cherries in a large jar, cover with brandy and leave for at least 15 days in a cool dark place.

2 Prepare the syrup by putting the sugar with 500ml/17fl oz/2 cups water in a pan over a medium heat. Let the sugar dissolve slowly, then bring to the boil until a syrup forms. Leave to cool, then add to the jar of cherries.

3 Now store again in a cool place for up to six weeks, out of the way of direct sunlight. Tip the jar upside down and give it a little shake every few days. When the liqueur is sweet and heady you can strain the liquid and transfer it into pretty bottles.

4 The cherries can be used as a topping for ice cream, but remember they are very alcoholic. Serve the liqueur in small glasses.

Energy 385kcal/1642kJ; Protein 1g; Carbohydrate 64g, of which sugars 64g; Fat 0g, of which saturates 0g; Cholesterol 0mg; Calcium 19mg; Fibre 2g; Sodium 4mg

Earthquake
Terremoto

Serves 4

1 litre/1³/₄ pints/4 cups white wine or pipeño

180ml/12 tbsp pineapple ice cream

40ml/8 tsp white sugar

40ml/8 tsp dark rum

Earthquakes are frequent in Chile and this drink was created in 1985 after a great movement that shook Santiago. Pipeño is a type of sweet fermented wine, and this is combined with rum to create a potent drink. After the first drink you are left with shaky legs, as if there has been a tremor.

1 Divide the white wine or pipeño between four large cocktail glasses.

2 Place 45ml/3 tbsp pineapple ice cream on top, then 10ml/2 tsp sugar and 10ml/2 tsp dark rum. Stir the mixture just before drinking.

Energy 274kcal/1138kJ; Protein 9g; Carbohydrate 11g, of which sugars 1.7g; Fat 21.9g, of which saturates 13.4g; Cholesterol 95mg; Calcium 83mg; Fibre 0.6g; Sodium 131mg

Serena-style papaya cocktail
Serena Libre

The Chilean papaya is the symbol of the city La Serena, where this drink was created in the 1990s. Papaya is not only delicious, it also contains a high amount of vitamin C. Combined with another local favourite, pisco, it makes a refreshing cocktail.

Serves 4

ice cubes

100ml/3¹/₂fl oz/scant ¹/₂ cup pisco

30ml/2 tbsp papaya juice

45ml/3 tbsp icing (confectioners') sugar

1 Put a few ice cubes, the pisco, papaya juice and sugar in a shaker. Shake vigorously for 30–45 seconds, until the mixture resembles a frappé. Strain into glasses and serve.

Below: Energy 41kcal/173kJ; Protein 0g; Carbohydrate 7g, of which sugars 7g; Fat 0g, of which saturates 0g; Cholesterol 0mg; Calcium 4mg; Fibre 0g; Sodium 2mg

Monkey's tail
Cola de mono

This delicious drink, with its strange name, is especially popular during the Christmas season, as well as for special occasions at other times of the year. It is made with Chilean brandy, milk, coffee, sugar and spices and served ice cold.

1 Put the milk, nutmeg, cinnamon and cloves in a pan over a medium heat and heat until boiling. Reduce the heat and simmer for 5 minutes to infuse with the spices.

2 Meanwhile, in a bowl, beat the egg yolks with the sugar until pale and thick. Remove the pan from the heat and gently stir the egg and sugar mixture into the milk. Return the pan to a low heat and cook, stirring, for 3 minutes more.

3 When the mixture has thickened slightly, remove the pan from the heat and add the coffee and brandy. Leave to cool.

4 Strain to remove the spices, and decant the cooled liquid into a sterilized bottle. Chill in the refrigerator until very cold.

5 Serve in glasses, with cinnamon sticks to stir. It will keep in the refrigerator for 2 days.

Serves 4

2.25 litres/3¾ pints/9 cups whole (full-fat) milk

2.5ml/½ tsp freshly ground nutmeg

2 cinnamon sticks, plus extra to garnish (optional)

5 cloves

3 egg yolks

60ml/4 tbsp white sugar

45ml/3 tbsp espresso coffee

275ml/9fl oz/generous 1 cup brandy

Energy 295kcal/1228kJ; Protein 4g; Carbohydrate 18g, of which sugars 18g; Fat 6g, of which saturates 3g; Cholesterol 159mg; Calcium 86mg; Fibre 0g; Sodium 32mg

Index